Architecture: action and plan

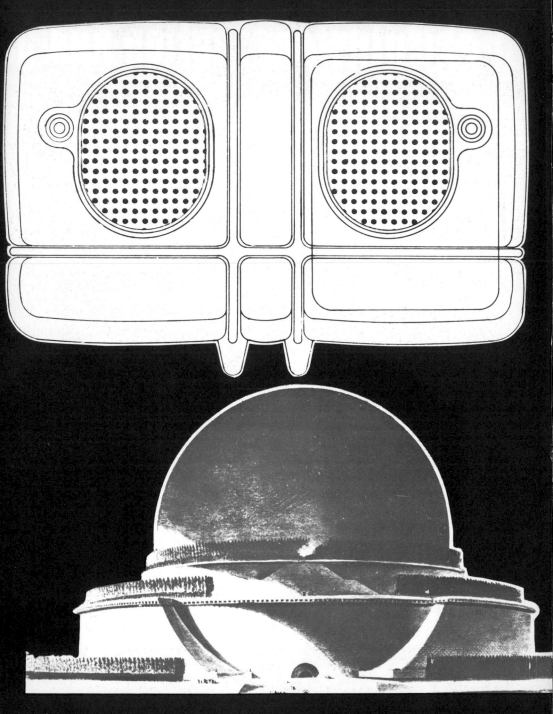

Architecture:
action and plan

Peter Cook

Studio Vista : London

Reinhold Publishing Corporation : New York

inside front cover: Illustration from Tchernikov's *101 Fantasies.*

page 1 : Henri Sauvage : housing project.
page 2 : Warren Chalk : 'capsule' home, elevation.
Etienne-Louis Boullée : Newton Cenotaph, 1784.

To Hazel, Warren, Dennis, David, Ron and Spider.

A Studio Vista/Reinhold Art Paperback
Edited by John Lewis
© Peter Cook 1967
Published in London by Studio Vista Ltd
Blue Star House, Highgate Hill, N 19
and in New York by Reinhold Publishing Corporation
a subsidiary of Chapman-Reinhold, Inc.
430 Park Avenue, New York
Library of Congress Catalog Card Number 67-14164
Set in 9/12 Univers Medium (Monotype Series 689)
Printed in the Netherlands
by N.V. Drukkerij Koch & Knuttel, Gouda

Architecture can be gauged by three criteria: performance, identity, and economy of means. Everyone has a subconscious or habitual way of recognising in buildings that are used every day symbols of comfort, familiar functions and occasionally, visual excitement. One aim of this book might be to extend this recognition, so that the cause and effect of these built symbols can be seen as deliberate, or at least relative. In gathering clues as to why parts of a building come to be where they are and how they are, we are opening Pandora's box. The game of question and answer, which is the only way to analyse a building of any quality, is at the same time one of the approved methods of architectural design; the variety of possible answers is the delight or the frustration of the process.

Recognising the clues is the first stage. Anticipating the questions is the second. Even within the space of this book though, one is attempting to use buildings which are inspiring rather than obvious. As any car enthusiast knows, the family saloon of the future is being proved now on the racetrack. The optimum can anyhow become banal by its very reasonableness, and most of our towns and cities have little inspiration behind their façades.

Standards of performance should not be static, and in this century an explosion of technological capacity means that we can build virtually anything we want. Every month there are a hundred new building materials available; every day the experience gained in space research, undersea exploration or dam building stretches the range of material further so that the choice of day-to-day environment can take advantage.

More simply, why have draughts if we can beat the heat barrier? A much better life has been made possible by those same efforts of extension and extreme which produced the new, weird buildings of thirty or forty years ago and constitute the hybrid sciences of the present; it is this that makes the present time most exciting for architecture. I hope that some of this excitement comes through. My strategy has been this: to keep the verbal interpretation simple and as timeless as possible, but to stress much further the imagery where otherwise it would fall into the same trap as does much of our environment — keeping safe, optimised, dull and dreary.

Economy of means does not equate with smallness of idea, barrenness of character. It is extremely difficult to design a simple-looking building. Equally, at the other end of the scale, the fruitiest Baroque is a superlative and therefore an attempt at an ideal. The search for absolutes lies behind most experimental or definitive architecture, and this is the thread which links the buildings illustrated.

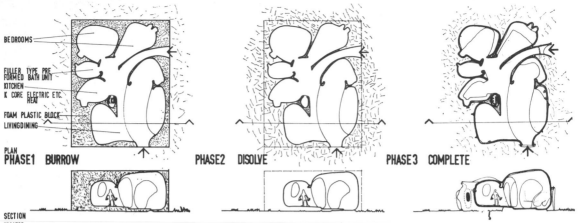

BEDROOMS

FULLER TYPE PRE FORMED BATH UNIT
KITCHEN
K CORE ELECTRIC ETC.
HEAT

FOAM PLASTIC BLOCK
LIVINGDINING

PLAN
PHASE1 BURROW　　　　　**PHASE2 DISOLVE**　　　　　**PHASE3 COMPLETE**

SECTION
PROJECT
PLASTIC SPRAY HOUSE

David Greene: Spray Plastic House, project, 1963.

bottom left: Air-inflated structure by ML Aviation.

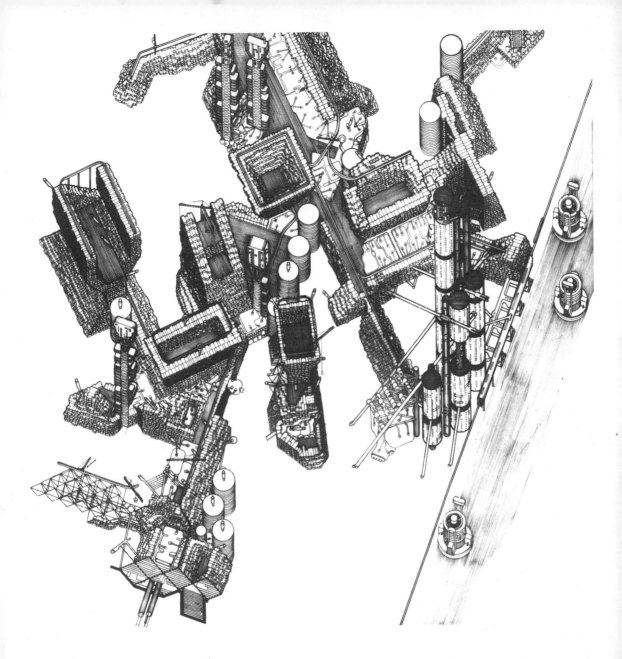

Peter Cook: 'Plug-in City', project, 1964, view from above.

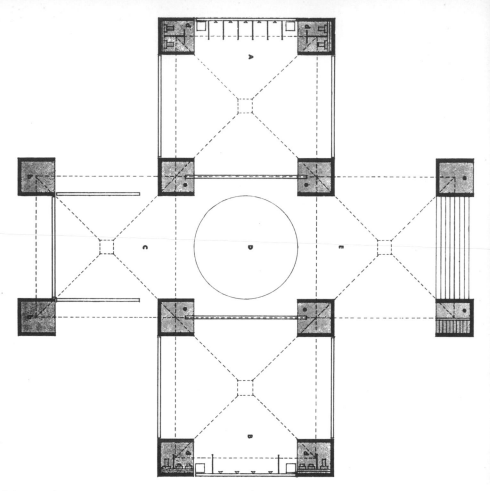

top: Louis Kahn : bath house, plan.
bottom: Stirling and Gowan : Selwyn College students'
rooms, plan.

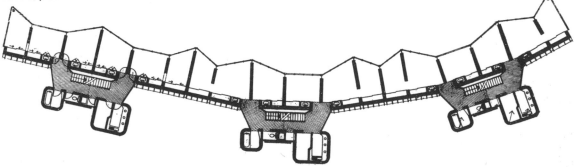

CHAPTER 1   ENVIRONMENT, REASON OR PURPOSE?

Using buildings is so regular an experience that we are quite happy to accept them for what they are — along with rain, sun, fire, water, and nowadays, the motor car. The last named shares with buildings the one difference from the list of inevitables: it is an artifact. It has been created by man to supplement the natural provisions of comfort and sustenance and has fulfilled this role so well that we now depend on it for survival. The motor car has achieved this position in seventy years, and even the more primitive wheeled devices which it replaced have a history which is shorter and in a much clearer line of development than architecture. Since shelter is a more passive activity than transport, since its exact requirements need to be adapted from place to place, since they reflect not only necessity but desire, their original (and still basic) function has been overlaid by an entanglement of overtones, progressions, restraints and hidden expedients.

We suddenly become aware of the building when it fails us. At such a time we ask questions: why does it leak? why should this room be too cold? why does that eyesore spoil the view? Perhaps just for a moment the intention of the designer makes direct contact and the entanglement of tradition and acceptance is pierced. It might at this point be easier if the question and answer were purely in terms of functional fulfilment. This cannot be so. Even in today's situation, when the layout and details of a building can be determined by a computer, the actual building so produced reflects the preferences and experiences of the computer's programmer. Even if we devised a design situation where subjective or 'personal' decisions could be virtually eliminated, the result would be open to an enormous range of possibilities, each multiplied by alternative materials, restrictions and mathematical sequences.

Even if the absolute were found it would not be enough. The distinction between architecture and mere shelter lies in the former's infinite ability to interpret basic (or less than basic) needs in some special way which accentuates them or conditions them so that they take on a greater relevance. At best, architecture gives experience a further dimension.

Over several thousand years the means by which architecture has been enriched have taken some strange turns : symbolism has taken over in a Stonehenge, a pyramid, or a gate that looks like a lion; but even the concept of elegance is itself probably little more than a respectable fantasy. Architecture is no different from any other discipline in constantly seeking absolutes and at the same time reacting from them. Architects have in their own way sought to find the absolute. From time to time it has seemed that Platonic ideals have been expressed in a piece of architecture. As with other disciplines, such absolutes have been more open to discussion when the example discussed is theoretical rather than actual. While architecture is essentially one of the practical arts, a philosophical tradition has in the past run beside or sometimes ahead of the contemporary output of buildings.

Recently, the real definition of what a building is, what a piece of material is, what is static, what is not static has been exploded by the total explosion of traditional concepts of matter and technology ; as with everything else any absolute may well be questioned in the future, even though it still holds good for the present. This fact acts more and more as a smoke screen for the comprehension of buildings, not only for people who have to live in them (but are not too worried about why a thing is as it is so long as it works), but for architects themselves. Quite clearly an analogy between architecture and other activities could be made by defining a sense of order which runs through them ; until 100 years ago, a layman could be initiated into the delights of architecture by first learning the rules — probably the Five Orders of architecture and the highlights of Classical Greece and Rome — and then reflecting upon the expertise with which the current exponent had interpreted them. If that exponent had deliberately chosen to flout the correct Classical use of the orders and entablatures, he would either revel in the romance of the thing or decry it as an 'outrage'. This is still the basis and level of lay criticism today. Though most intelligent laymen would admit that the forms of Classical architecture or any revivalist style are no longer appropriate to present needs, there is a strong instinct for direction : a feeling that it is only the styling that needs to be different and that a sense of pure order can be re-defined in very much the traditional terms.

If this is not so, is there any such thing as architecture left? If the original motives have disappeared and the contexts may well do so in the future, there must be an alternative; the act of making an architectural decision can perhaps be stripped of its mystique, while some far more viable set of operations is seen to add up to something — not a style, not even a discipline, but some indefinable aggregate of operations which have been intelligent and appropriate and have given a situation its fourth dimension.

A building does not exist only within itself; each one, without becoming a miniature essay in Town Planning, reflects life going on outside. Decisions in design have reflected the prejudices and necessities of whatever society produced the need for them.

There have been traditional hierarchies of life: Medieval society, for instance, conveniently divided itself into the Church, the State, the Manor and the Home. The attitude to the provision of shelter followed a parallel hierarchy. Churches not only expressed a metaphysical analogy by soaring up to Heaven and offering the drama of moving from a small dark doorway into a tall light nave, but exercised the maximum effort within the technology of the day. Small-scale sculpture and large-scale engineering were combined, and the total effort became more than just a correct juxtaposition of parts: it had the quality of assertion, of a singular idealism. There may be an argument here for agreeing with the nineteenth-century Gothicists (though for non-romantic reasons), that Renaissance architecture is inappropriate for churches, since the disciplines of a Classical style depend upon the equation and balancing-out of a set of inter-dependent parts — there is nothing very singular about this; it is reasonable rather than assertive.

The State built in order to subjugate or in order to impress. The motives are simple: the Tower of London relies upon basic engineering and strategic planning; in the terms of the day, no expense would be spared to ensure that a castle could withstand the enemy or even the population immediately surrounding it. Later the distinction from within to without is less violent, but there remains the basic necessity to create quite a different form of environment. This instinct has survived into this century, when even the democratisation of power retains the idea of awe and pomp in buildings that represent authority, Civic Centres are still built of expensive materials, with lavish space standards in ceremonial rooms and the traditional devices of a tower, an obelisk or large clock — a hangover from the time when such a thing was necessary to maintain a defence of the stronghold, and to remind the townsfolk who was boss. There is even perhaps a hint of paternalism in the nineteenth-century Town Hall Clock in an age when most people have watches.

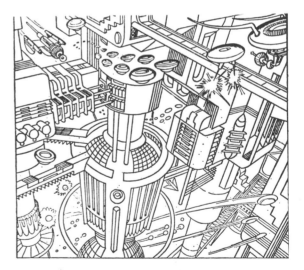

'Then I saw — great towers — architectural leviathons that launched into skies where two suns burned brightly in a solar system far from our own! I was in the world of the saucer creature — whose race was obviously superior to the men of earth! The sight was staggering and filled me with awe!' (original caption from space-comic).

A 'cottage ornée' (from Papworth's *Rural Residences* 1818).

Significantly, in every age the more 'important' buildings are able to distinguish themselves from the rest by some means or other. In areas where there is stone, the courses are laid in a much more sophisticated way. In areas where there is no stone, the common dwellings, and even public buildings, are of the indigenous material while the Church and the Manor are built of stone, brought up river. The Manor often has further overtones: not always a miniature castle or palace, it may well be the reverse; although basically formed in the same way as the local cottages and of the same basic components, it is scaled-up; it has more rooms and higher roofs; it is an aggregate cottage. The Victorian romantics discovered the delights of such buildings along with Gothic architecture, so that Compton Wynates becomes reinterpreted as a *cottage orné*.

It is in some ways simplest to find a connection between pure functionalism and architectural expression in the humblest order of the hierarchy, yet even here an enormous range of diversion can come from a preference for one kind of window rather than another or from the carrying on of a tradition long after its origins have been lost to view. This results in some extraordinary cases of pseudo-morphology, such as happened when the early motor car retained the form and paraphenalia necessary when it was being pulled by a horse. In houses, this is often known to be ridiculous, but is nevertheless desired. You do not have to go far to find baronial chimney-breasts or pseudo half-timbering. Such things have for long been the butt of thinking architects, yet they genuinely reflect an important part of the basis for any building's existence — desirable 'overtones' as well as desirable function. The only answer is to achieve such an integration of the building's real desirability and the enjoyment of this, that a substitute 'image' becomes unnecessary.

Power station control room (late 1920's).

The fundamental problem in enclosing space is finding the means of holding it up. The simplest way in a primitive culture seemed to be the scooping out of earth or the piling up of stones. Both methods simulated the naturally-found cave structure. It is important to reflect that successive generations of builders have first of all looked at the existing situation, however faulty, and only when this fails them have they extended to the full their technological ingenuity. Even in the periods when taste and intellectual reasoning have been highly developed (High Greek, the Renaissance and our own), the first instincts of a designer have been in traditional terms. This business of tradition and its overthrow has been seen at certain key times as a battle of fundamentals. During the nineteenth century in England the polemic was between the Classical and Gothic (or 'Romantic') wings of architecture. Its resolution was the negation of the ideals of both groups in a period (around the 1900s) of heady eclecticism and free for all in which many of her landmarks — Piccadilly Circus, Regent Street, most of Windsor Castle — were styled. The idealism of the 1920s in Europe found expression in the Great Battle for the Modern. Most buildings which go up today are claimed to have their roots in this so-called 'modern' architecture, which surely never envisaged its fruit as the majority of City office blocks and 'developments' among which we are forced to live. Yet the styling is there; the horizontal window, the large, flat areas of glass, a blank white wall: these can be recognised by any layman as the look of modern architecture.

If we analyse the plan of a typical mainstream building and strip it of its styling — ignoring whether there is a strip window or a series of mullioned bays, whether it is stone or expanded polystyrene, blank and smooth or embossed and crenellated — we find the usual features.

There is something in the middle or something at the end by which you enter; something on the corner to catch your eye; a more elaborate organisation at the bottom of the building than the top, on the traditional assumption that more is happening round this part of the building. (A device like that used in Renaissance palaces, where this important strata is one floor up, is a typical sophistication of one of the highly developed periods). A more realistic attitude to the conflict between tradition and modernity is to regard the latter as a state of mind which gives equal consideration to the whole range of methods and ideas (including those not thought of before), rather than reiterating the 'accepted method' of the day. In this way we get better buildings by continually broadening the range of architectural method. Such a situation would at the same time undermine 'tradition' as a blinkered, narrow line, and reinforce it as an accumulation of ideas seen over the widest range in methods and the deepest range in time, both backwards and forwards.

From its indigenous origins the art of building has acquired the same sort of mystique about how things are put together as several other craft traditions. Just as the crafts which back up architecture are indivisible from the other useful crafts – carpentry, boat-building, plastering, easel painting — and these overlap with the fine arts, so the mystique of design is intertwined with the business of the craft. The medieval architects are known to have been master masons. Yet where does the obvious sophistication of thinking behind a Henry Yvele differ from mere knowledge? Only in the nineteenth century did the romance of 'craft' rather than industry crop up as an intellectual ideal. Until this time craft methodology was only desirable if appropriate.

There is no such problem in pre-wheel civilisations. The significance of the effort required to transport a non-local material has already been mentioned. From the reproduction of the cave came the business of choice. Presumably a large cave had certain advantages over a small one: the piling up of stones becomes less tedious if large stones rather than small ones are used. It is only a short step to the 'invention' of the lintel; technology has arrived. Artifacts such as the lintel, the window (first as a mere opening), the stringing of one chamber along with another — either as a rationalisation of the privacy problem by dividing up a single unit, or more probably in the first instance the agglomeration of several dwellings close together for protection — (this last is after all the basis of planning) — the placing together of various functions in one organisation whilst retaining the ability to separate them. With this last device sophistication had arrived.

It would have been possible to continue the development of an architecture on such logical and evolutionary principles for ever. It is interesting to speculate on what the state of architecture would be now. But the creation of architecture is a human invention and the waywardness of its development has as a result at many points a human lack of logic. The first buildings which are credited with discussion are already human playthings. The excercise of preference for its own sake is used to embellish a piece of basic thinking. The underground tomb made up of successive chambers has shapes and undulations of profile which deliberately draw attention to one part rather than the other, although the basic elements are similar to each other. Symbolism is very deeply related to preferential designing, as we have already discovered. In addition to

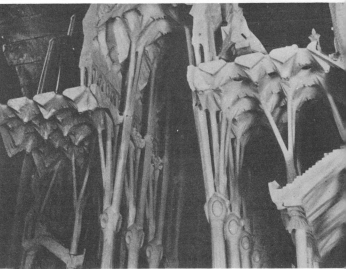

15

PROGNOSES OF THE FUTURE FROM THE PAST:
Set from the film 'Metropolis'.

Overleaf:
THE FLUENCY OF STRUCTURE:
above: Isfahan, Friday Mosque.
below left: spray plastic skinning.
below right: Gaudi: structural model of the nave and aisles of the Sagrada Familia church: an experimental and virtuoso extension of the Gothic section.

the extreme loaded values of important building versus hovel, the more subtle manipulations probably take up more of the time of every known architect and certainly form the substance of professional criticism.

The basic principles of structure are as direct as other physical laws. Lumps of material usually rest one upon the other; more rarely they are hung; they can be poised in thin air if we rely upon the consistency of their substance. Modern architecture is credited with gymnastic demonstrations of the 'look no hands!' variety, but the instinct for this was alive before the invention of reinforced concrete — (the seven wonders of the world consisted of the largest, tallest, widest and so on). Without the show-off instinct we should not have a Taj Mahal or a Great Pyramid. In modern architecture, this demonstration of the ability to create a new image which appears to defy the limits of reason (or perhaps just tradition) has been central to the creation of an idea of breakthrough. Concrete is able to effect an enormous cantilever; space uncluttered by columns has close connotations with mechanical simplicity; glass has more power than any other material so far discovered to achieve all things to all men. The simple manipulation of cave-to-cave becomes infinitely subtler: to see but not to be part of, to be visually part of but climatically insulated, to reduce the nature of matter down to a hair line yet still to be able to make it work for you — and to make it (almost) unseen — this is the stuff of civilisation. It was as great a breakthrough as powered flight in psychological as well as physical terms.

In the mainstream there has been a continual back and forth between expressive manipulation and the hand to mouth tradition of necessary craft and engineering. Every so often there is a loudly expressed cry for a return to 'honesty' in architecture. On closer examination this is seen to be the imposition of certain restraints upon the number of manipulations made in design, with references back to certain (selected) historical models of parts and technical gambits. The surprising thing, which lay people are quicker to discover than the more partisan architect, is that these restraints usually have more to do with the styling involved than the actual honesty of function. What might be called 'natural engineering' is still open-ended enough to stimulate our experience. Again we need breadth of vision to recognise it.

The important contribution of the image, and of the long tradition of forward-looking 'gestural' architecture, has been in its explosion of dried-up thinking. The further back we delve, the more difficult it is to sort out the cause and effect of such designs. The experience of the great composers of music is better documented: here it has become almost a pre-requisite of greatness to shock at the first hearing. Certainly there are many projects for buildings in the category of the 'fantastic' which have anticipated events. By the seventeenth century, the concept of the ideal city could be put forward by a visionary-like Ledoux with one foot in the philosophical traditions of Utopia and the other in his own need to create new architecture. Utopianism is closely bound to the physical environment by Robert Owen's time (early nineteenth century) and the term itself has been transferred to any wayout architectural project.

From the infinite choice of parts to create the image, there remain some which have the power or overtones of the total concept and are therefore the natural choice as means to the end. Stone posessed the strength to achieve height and form and was the obvious choice for the building of a cathedral. Now that we have a million materials to build with, most of us would prefer a stainless steel window frame to a painted and galvanised one. It would have the sophistication, precision and specification appropriate to a machine civilisation: the overtones can be brought right down to the choice of the door handle.

Why is Le Corbusier's famous remark about a house as 'machine for living in' so often quoted at us? Undoubtedly it was an important image-statement for the functionalists — form follows function; the twenties had an infinitely simpler dictum than the nineteenth century values for architecture of 'firmness, commodity and delight'.

But there have been many other equally significant catch-phrases in modern architecture. It is the abrasiveness of the machine as an image which remains when it is applied to that most comfortable of traditional values, the home. The edgy way in which the phrase must have been received at the time takes us back again to the craft/honesty situation. We have recently passed through a resurgence of delight in so-called 'natural' materials.

Against this we have the idea that technology can now provide most of the answers to problems of design; the ideal is a single range of prefabricated parts for all building situations. An attractive idea in the abstract, it ignores a fundamental facet of design: that it exists in the dimension of time as well as space. Our life and ways of using things change year by year, and nowadays our means of solving problems change month by month. The architecture of the technological age is not simple. Nevertheless architects are becoming divided between a so-called 'technological' architecture of standard posts, panels and metal trusses, and the hand-made architecture which seems to demand natural wood finishes, bricks that really look lumpy and clay-like, and concrete that makes the most of shuttering joints and so on. In fact, neither type of building is particularly valid for a current set of situations. The most honest expression might include some components which are standardised and run off in a factory and others which are very obviously custom-built on site. The tragedy is that such buildings usually lack discipline of design and detail, which is much more easily achieved by defining and restraining the choice of methods; a decision to prefabricate the lot, or to build all walls in brick, produces consistency.

Evolving levels of consistency is the second fundamental problem of design, after that of creating experience. There remains the instinct for following the rules which is expected of good buildings. But marvellous things have been created which break the so-called rules constantly — what of the false façades of the Taj Mahal? What of the rendering of rubble and brickwork in many of the classic-modern buildings of the 'thirties to simulate the machine-image flat, white surface of concrete? After all most cathedrals are the agglomeration of several styles cheek by jowl. Inconsistency between what a thing represents and what it is constitutes a serious breaking of rules; so too does using more than one answer to one problem.

How do we recognise great architecture? Is it the ruthlessness of the consistency? Obviously this is not always so. Yet as a method of design it is reasonable to maintain a consistent attitude to problems which are the same or analogous. The detailing of a window frame will be similar to the frame of a door, and in the same building may actually have the same profile — this

Montezuma's Castle, Verde Valley, Arizona.

seems reasonable. But then a window needs to keep out rain and ice, and this is not required of an internal door which may need to keep out a draught. Furthermore, the door of a cupboard may need far less strength than a much-used room door, so that to make their frame dimensionally the same is not strictly to practise the correct economy of means. But economy of means is inherent in the idea of consistency. This rather domestic example may seem to be easily solved by common sense — you 'switch off' your strict sense of aptitude at one end, or economy at the other, or lean over backwards to find analogies: all openings are similar, whether window, door or coal-hole, so let's make them the same. Is this consistency? Yet if every solution of a problem is a separate and tailor-made item, the whole building will not only be expensive but aesthetically and logically ridiculous. One's eye could not rest on any line, since everything which was different would set up an 'occurence'. The architect who can place analogous problems in the right design categories is halfway towards evolving a building of sense — and therefore probably a building of style as well.

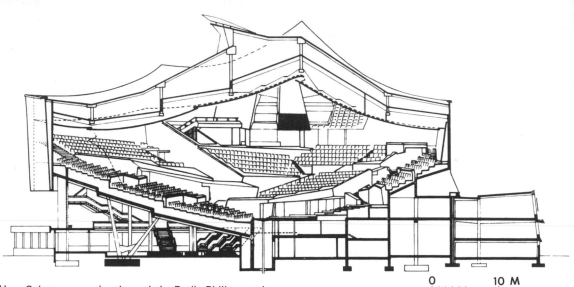

Hans Scharoun : section through the Berlin Philharmonie.

0   10 M

A subtle distinction exists between 'good' architecture and 'great' architecture. As a part of life 'great' things are necessary : an environment made up of sensible answers to necessary problems would be intolerable. This has been a little-stated failure of New Towns, where most of the buildings and almost all of the housing is sensible within its terms of reference, but the total environment is dull. The social in-balance and 'wrongness' of the London slums had colour, and the architecture reflected this exactly. Where now are the gin palace and the alley? Of course artificial attempts to recreate such things misfire embarrassingly. Great architecture is often confused with impressiveness; are cathedrals necessarily designed at a higher level of artifice than all parish churches? Stimulation by architecture has also an in-built time dimension; the circle of fashion is as marked in buildings as it is in fine art, writing and clothes. The turnover is necessarily slower than *haute couture*, but the revival of interest

in Victorianism (for whatever reasons) is symptomatic of this colouring of critical levels by taste.

As any building must have the necessary framework of structure within it to maintain itself in one piece, much of our discussion here concerns preference and embellishment. Even if a building leaks or offends the eye, this is to some extent marginal. We can bung up the leak or change the window frame; we can paint the building or wait until it becomes fashionable once more. It is more difficult to maintain its existence if it is falling down. There are such famous cases as Winchester Cathedral, resting on a raft of logs of wood. When this was discovered a technique of 'grouting' with concrete was evolved. Many ecclesiastic buildings now contain grouted foundations, 'stone' columns that are now more concrete than stone, spires which have had the wooden framework painstakingly replaced by a concrete lattice. Yet this whole category is an exception, since the

A vision of industry and structural dynamic (from Tchernikov's *101 Fantasies).*

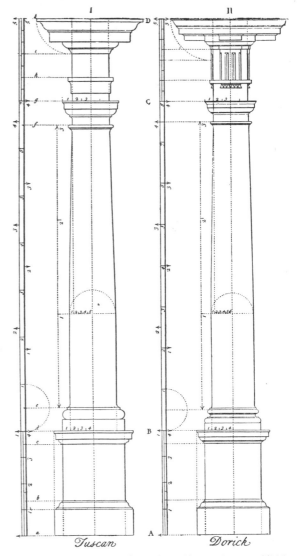

The Tuscan and Doric orders (from James Gibb's *Rules for Drawing the Several Parts of Architecture).*

intrinsic value of such buildings makes it necessary to falsify the original physical situation.

Beneath the surface, most buildings conform to a relatively small number of basic structural gambits. After the cave comes the chamber. The outside walls eventually become separated, structurally, from the roof. The lintel becomes extended and refined until it becomes a beam. The wall becomes similarly refined until it need only occur where a beam is resting on it, and then we have a new component: the column. At this point there is an important breakthrough: structure and enclosure are no longer dependent on total mass. A framework of columns and beams can be infilled or not infilled as required. The manipulation of frame and infill is the point at which basic structure and embellishment meet.

The development of the corbel, which is a refinement of the wall (but in some ways not so far from the 'cave' and the pile of stones),

Kidwelly Castle. *(Crown copyright)*

produced the dome and eventually the vault. Thereby the strict 'rule' that an enclosure,though no longer dependent on mass, was still defined by the limits of the post and lintel cage, was broken; a dome can span a dimension far beyond that of most beams. These three devices are still in many ways the basis of the structure of most buildings. The invention of reinforced concrete and, earlier, that of iron and steel have extended the range, but have not materially revised the theory. Buildings are solid, (the solid is nowadays often aggregated in honeycomb construction); post-and-beam, (the frameworks possible with present technology are often complex in the extreme and use three-dimensional transference of forces in many directions, but the lintel started it all); and arched or bowed. Concrete has now

achieved such strength with its reinforcement of steel that dams of enormous girth are commonplace. Pre-fabrication relies largely on frame structure, since its parts break down into primary (frame) and secondary (infill); such demarcation can be very appropriate to the needs of standardisation.

From time to time architects have maintained a sort of love-hate relationship with the world of engineering. For the last two hundred years it has been possible to employ an 'architect' and an 'engineer' as distinct creative designers with a demarcation line drawn between them. In many cases the role of the architect has been to embellish by means of an approved crust of styled material round the edges of the basic engineering structures. It has followed that in retrospect the buildings of the nineteenth cent-

Johannes Duiker: Open-air school, Amsterdam, 1930.

ury which are most admired by modern architects are those in which pure engineering only is involved, such as the more direct of the railway termini with their pure and yet exciting roofs, cast iron bridges, warehouses these are not considered worth the cost of 'architecture'. At another level the love-hate relationship is expressed in the difference between the attitudes of engineers and architects, which arises out of their training. The one discipline has a pragmatic bias, the other an intuitive. At the highest level such differences disappear, but many buildings around us still bear the marks of this lack of communication of intention between the two people most responsible for the forms of our environment. Another aspect of the relationship follows on from the intuitive approach of most architects, who retreat from what they feel to be a lack of sensitivity in day-to-day engineering. The concept of the building has to be adjusted (perhaps limited?) against necessities of structure. This may be passing; in history many of the great advances in concept have manifested themselves in gestures with an engineering image.

In the third basic category, the arched, the spatial explosion within a domed room founded the Byzantine churches, the Pantheon, the Baths of Caraccalla. With Gothic architecture, there was a rarification of arch and frame in a structure of true dynamism: vaults, enormous windows and, greatest of all, the flying buttress. Later architecture is much more a story of the absorption of new materials. The adaptation of the immediately preceding method, which we have found to be a basis of tradition, is certainly

above : Charles Voysey : 'The Homestead' Frinton, 1905. In its stripping-down of traditional parts, Voysey's work can be regarded as the rationalist end of the English Romantics, or the beginning of the 'moderns'. It is certainly its former overtones that have appealed as a model to the more indulgent developers of houses in the 1920's and 30's.

below : Ionel Schein, Yves Magnent and R. A. Coulon : motel cabin in reinforced plastics : designed for mobility, mass production and stacking plus a high level of servicing.

true of this phase. The very first moves in the language of a new material are cautious, but when its potential really begins to be understood the whole thing becomes more creative and more exciting. As we have seen, modern architecture without concrete is rather phoney, but more than this, it springs from the gesture of 'look what it can do'. Steel and glass have produced not only buildings which use these materials exclusively, but which represent man's control over environment. At such a stage the handling of substance steps very far beyond mere craftsmanship.

If we take the inflatable skin structure, which is a symbol of architecture at the present extreme of technology, we can regard it as the end-point of refinement of our basic operations, or science fiction come true. The structure depends on thin air to maintain pressure and so does the position of the skin. The skin itself is infinitesimal in thickness : when deflated the whole building folds up into almost nothing ; the building can be here — or not here ; it can be hung, tethered, floated. Yet it can be seen as only the latest stage of the sophistication of the arched form ; the most recent mouldable material ; another variant of the chamber. Significantly it embraces both tradition and the extension of our knowledge of method, and is also exciting. To uncover the reasoning behind a design one must try to understand the psychology of most architecture. The hybrid state which architecture now assumes — the architect as *uomo universale* with a creative ability to absorb aesthetics, sociology, science, economics, art, plumbing and the rest — is not very old. It was simpler when the mainstream architect could buy a manual of the 'Rules of Architecture', which consisted of the five classical orders and other necessary details of classical form, so that any building could be clothed in a style according to formula. This naturally enough ignored the fact already discussed, that great buildings break rules, and that stylistic formula is not design. Nevertheless a doorway in an English market town could simulate a discipline that had its origins in ancient Greece. People made the Grand Tour to the sites of Classical antiquity in Greece and Rome and began to record the appearance of archetypal buildings in enormous editions with which we are all familiar: exquisite engravings of elevations, sections and plans. High Italian Renaissance was similarly transmitted to England, and from Inigo Jones onwards the local product of sufficient imagination began. Interpretation was still hindered unless one developed the ability to see past the rule book. This seemed to be possible if one made the Tour oneself, and the method of induction has survived until this century when the teaching of architecture and some formalising of theories could diversify. Nevertheless, the latest building of a Corbusier (if you happen to live in Europe) or a Louis Kahn (if you happen to live in America) results in a rash of student visits, with the camera replacing the engraver's needle.

If the mainstream has always needed accepted archetypes, the avant-garde has seen its task as creating them. The time-lag between creation and acceptance by the mainstream has diminished from centuries (if we count Ancient Greece as a model for the Renaissance) to about two years for a fashionable architect. The early Renaissance situation was as much the rebirth of culture as a whole from the darkness of the Dark Ages, as it was a re-use of the various orders, entablatures and mouldings. This inter-identity of formal detail associated with a culture remains with us today. Modern architecture derives very much from the political and social dynamic implicit in the creation of 'people's housing' — the assertion of the proletariat and breakdown of the old hierarchy with homestead at the bottom. Le Corbusier's *Vers Une Architecture*, which explains the concept of house as machine, makes much play of pictures of automobiles and ships. There is power in the superhuman scale of a gridded façade and the gigantic scale of Constructivist buildings. It is not just on formal grounds that Peter Behrens' AEG powerhouse remains one of the archetypes for young architects. The conquest of space and of the world underwater have similar creative associations now.

However valid or invalid these associations of ideas are, they have pushed architectural experiment forward by the roundabout way of feeding off the cultural situation in other fields. At the same time there is the more watertight, more academic pursuit of architectural archaeology. This continuously looks to antiquity and the architectures of the past to find absolutes — lessons in problem solving which are universal. From time to time a new 'discovery' is made, whereby the planning of a Greek town or the proportion of an early Christian church is seen to contain formal thinking which can be used today. The problem with this process is that it is less reliable than fact and is almost always coloured by the researcher's own preferences. However interesting abstract theorising about buildings may be, it is extremely dangerous without constant recourse to the form and appearance and mechanics of the building itself. Most of all it is valueless without some knowledge of the means available at the time (and whether they were fully exploited); this is the real stuff of architecture.

A scale of values can now be attempted. If we discount the traditional 'importance of building

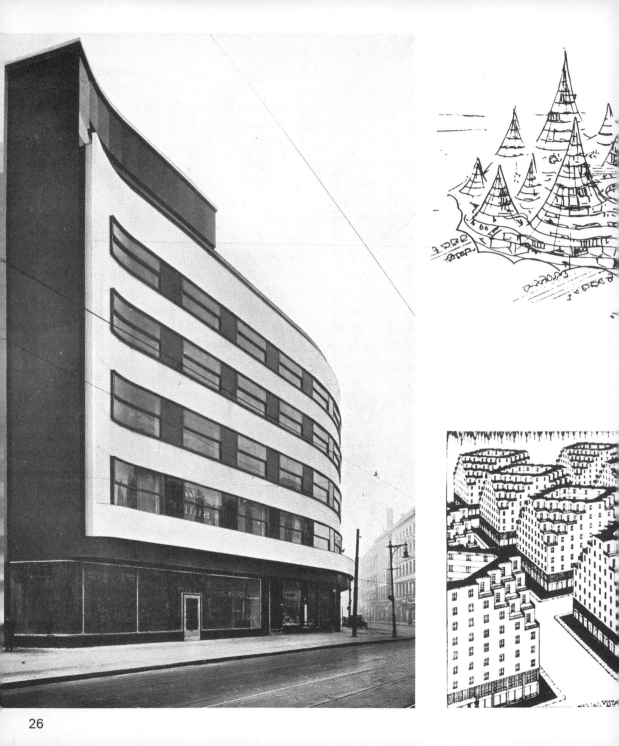

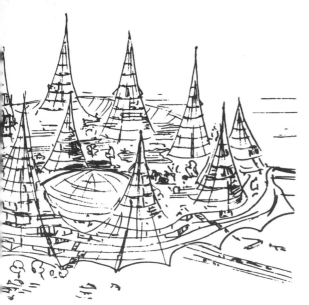

left: Luckhardt brothers and Alfonso Anker: Teschow Haus, Berlin, c. 1925.
above: Frei Otto: Project for a town covered by lightweight tent skinning: conditioned environment. c. 1960.
below: Piero Portaluppi: Monte Amarillo Quarter, 1920: a neo-futurist extension of the traditional filled-block-between-streets.

type' hierarchy, as we must, every building represents an effort to be made at the highest and most absolute level. Is this thinking possible? The tendency is to regard the single building as less and less of an entity in itself. This is not only the outcome of planning legislation, but of urban thinking as a whole. Every man his castle is not necessarily a good idea any longer, but even if it were, one building's needs cannot be imposed on another. Building is now much more for the good of the community — a cultural and political by-product; 'environment' is there to be enjoyed by all, and by 'amenity' we mean a communal facility, so our building must be seen in context, both from the point of view of planning and aesthetics. If these are constraints, we have somehow to eradicate them from positive decision-making.

Grouping of forces is pretty basic to anything larger than a single cell. Subjectivity creeps in from here on. The more potentially 'interesting' rooms or groups of rooms are given the 'treatment'; if that hurdle is passed we arrive at the contrapuntal device of 'cage' and 'box'. If we take the 'cage' as representing the network of access or structure and the 'box' as representing the unit of control, the method seems to hold good over an enormous range. In a city plan the cage is made up of streets, rivers, railways; the boxes are blocks or even individual buildings. In a school, the cage is the corridor network, the boxes mostly classrooms. The idea works vertically in some cases: the tower block of dwellings has a cage formed by light and view on the perimeter, corridor and lift shaft, rubbish chute, escape in the centre, the box naturally being the dwelling. Even in medieval planning, the cage of a church can easily be seen as the line of columns separating nave and aisle in one direction, crossing and

27

Arata Isozaki (member of the Japanese 'metabolist' group): city structure c. 1964. Quotation: 'Only one thing is certain: the future will contain the ruins of the present'.

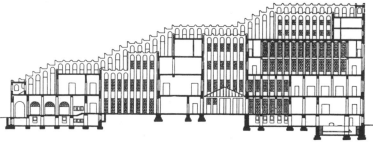

Hans Poelzig: Friendschaft Building, Istanbul (section): an expressionist interpretation of very dense, courtyard planning.

transepts in the other; the boxes are here flowing into each other, but are nevertheless clearly defined both spatially and liturgically. On a much smaller scale, an analogy between the cage-and-box definition can be seen in service and served spaces, but this is a refinement which can be discussed later.

It will be seen that within the box itself there will be quite an ebb and flow of activities. This smaller circuit is itself a planning problem and can have the same overtones and complications as the whole building, but taken as a later stage of consideration it simplifies the design of one's own building or the analysis of someone else's. A good cage organisation should somehow suggest itself when one wanders through a building and should certainly come through strongly when one reads a plan or section drawing. Confusion starts if it breaks its own rhythm. If a staircase suddenly starts to climb more steeply one is subconsciously disturbed. If a cage system chops and changes its method of reference to the other parts we become confused. It is likely that the geometry of the cage will be consistent, which is, of course, a start.

At this point the subordination of the ideals of one area to the simplicity of the whole crops up again. The cage system may in some cases be so strong that the boxes are very much its infill rather than appendages. Many contemporary buildings have made such a strong analogy between organisational cage and structural cage that the frame and the bay dominate the whole — this is not so very different from the Classical form, in which the columnic rhythm is by far the strongest component.

If some more local unit of space is seen as the next stage, this also suggests that it is increasingly influenced by its environment. It is likely that its use is specific and that the people who use it identify very much with its atmosphere. Just as its organisation may well be more cyclic than linear, so too it may be more loaded than balanced out. The whole box may be complementary rather than similar to the other boxes, but within its precise definitions of form and use it can be more or less irritating. Design at this level becomes much more a matter of ergonomics. We all know how much a living-room space can be affected by a change-round of furniture; this is psychological, though the components are the same. With most buildings the walls and doors and other points at which we constantly touch the building and look at it are as close but are immovable. Much of today's thinking and building is concerned with trying to design a flexible architecture of moving parts, changeable parts and, soon, disposable parts. In this way the artificial restraint of solidity which is a left-over of the past could disappear.

When it comes to the component hardware itself we are faced with hardly any discipline except statics. So long as we remain aware of the existence of matter and therefore of objects, these objects need to be maintained only for as long as we need them. It has often been said in this century that there is no basic difference between architecture and industrial design. At the other end of the scale it can be seen that there is little difference between the design of a city and that of a house. The criteria of design are largely those of aptitude first, and clarity of organisation second, but the romantic in us need not really take fright at this seeming insensitivity, because everybody has a different interpretation of even the words 'clarity' and 'organisation'. Not only this: as the choice of methods becomes greater and greater (and our present technology suggests that it does), the range of interpretation widens too.

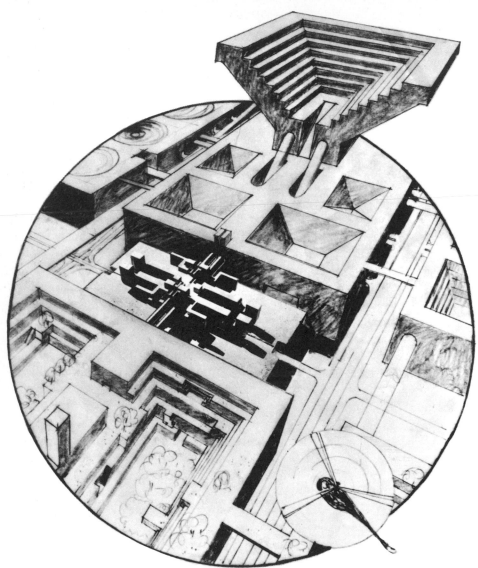

Hans Hollein: City.

As architecture is a social art the value of a building must lie chiefly in its ability to create environment out of human situations. The architect can, if he wishes, set himself the limit of the existing pattern. A block of flats can be designed with exactly those standards of space, light, density and atmosphere that its tenants have been used to elsewhere, but most good architects would not be content with this. This is not arrogance, but a response to the challenge that a building is not just fabric: it is the extension of the human body.

As we have seen in other ways, architecture which is the product of any society reflects in its form the prejudices of that society. In ideal terms the architect regards his building as the embodiment of a social ideal. Sometimes this is the product of the accepted norm; in experimental buildings this is more often an embodiment of 'the new life'.

We have seen that medieval society was far from co-ordinated, and the history of the last four hundred years has been a series of explosions towards emancipation. The architecture which runs parallel does reflect this, but somehow smooths out the bumps. The tradition of looking backwards has much to do with this. If we take the development of the dwelling as an example, we find no clear break from hovel to cottage, cottage to large, multi-roomed cottage, and from this to the two-storey local authority dwelling. Space standards improve, certain archetypes (such as the two-up-two-down) emerge, but the social pattern has far greater force in the town planning which carries them.

Renaissance society still maintained much of the medieval. The rebirth of learning and the realisation of so many new sophistications was the province of the rich and the educated; their palaces and seminaries could demand and design a new architecture. The planning of cities reflected their tastes, and so the dwellings were adapted to the cage form allotted to them, but did not absorb the new sophistications quickly. The diversification of building types which emerged during the eighteenth and nineteenth centuries naturally enough borrowed from above: the workhouse and the fire station still had much in common stylistically with the palaces, though they had somehow to evolve their own organisational form. Even this was submerged for a long period; there is in all our mind's eyes the image of the 'public building', not any one sort of public building, just a public building — generally in a Classical style.

Strangely, more has been contributed to the development of architecture by the snob instinct and the cachet than by the humble and traditional. The merchant of the seventeenth century, wishing to assume some of the refinements of the traditionally rich, took a close look at their architecture. What then started as embellishment, such as a columned portico attached to the large, otherwise medieval house, developed further. A grand salon and a heightening of the main storey, if only to allow for the addition of pilasters, led to an eventual change in the organisation. The chain reaction down the social scale led to the eventual metamorphosis of towns and cities. Later the concept of the 'villa' makes

Mies van der Rohe: Lake Shore Apartments, Chicago, 1957.

Typical London terrace of the early 19th century.

an even greater change. The emergence of a middle class directly forced the assumption of an independence of environment out of all proportion to reality. The villa with its own plot of land and own identity (ideally surrounded by open air, or at least 'semi-detached') naturally had to have the details of the rich man's dwelling.

below : Peter Cook: 'Mound' project, 1964 : a multi-use centre, inward-looking and covered with grass banks.

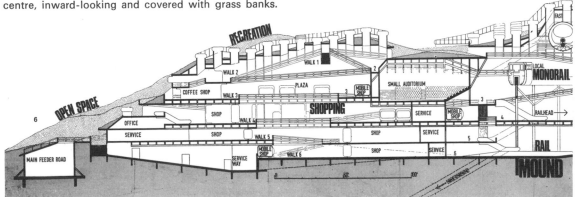

Town planning, from being something imposed by those in control, developed into a tool that could capitalise these aspirations. It became desirable to provide a network that could absorb the 'town house' (the most natural of the developments from traditional housing) and the 'villa'. Surprisingly and frighteningly, the latter is still with us; the ribbon of single dwellings is part of Western society. Even the famous concept of Ebenezer Howard's 'Garden City', which can be traced through to the nineteenth-century Romantic movement, results in a reinforcement of the estate-of-villas. The desired overtone of the Garden City and Garden Suburb was a return to the simplicity (and of course the factual form) of the village and the cottage, with everyone growing their own vegetables and enjoying sun, light and air. Meanwhile, a stratification of human contact has grown up round our developing institutions to replace the old social order. As new facilites and occupations become more sophisticated, they evolve traditions, images and even languages. As we enter a bank, with its required aura of dignity and solidity, we enter a separate world from the street outside; the architect has created the appropriate shell for this atmosphere. 'Institutional' is a particular word of condemnation, yet we cling to recognition of building types just as we cling to social groupings of one kind or another. As one transfers from one atmosphere to another one is experiencing a kind of architecture. Yet the self-consciousness of it has its own danger of phoney-ness.

left: Johannes Duiker: Zonnestraal Sanatorium, Hilversum, 1928.

above: G. P. Goltz, M. P. Parusnikoff and S. N. Kojin: factory building, Moscow, c. 1926, typical of the highly developed and organized yet dynamic architecture of the Russian post-constructivists.

Paul Rudolph: Car Park, New Canaan: styled to give a much stronger imagery than the engineering actually demands.

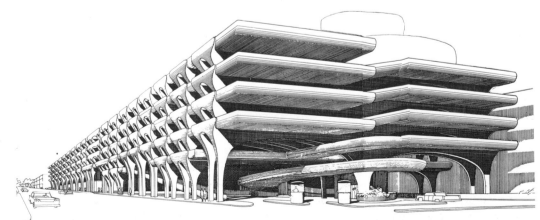

The wider technological range and intellectual questioning in the study of architecture has begun to take effect in the creative use of sociology in designing buildings. Few areas of urban renewal would now be attempted without a social survey of some kind. More positively, analogies are now being drawn between patterns of living and circumstance and their possible architectural organisation. It is now recognised that the closeness of ancient towns, where one activity runs cheek by jowel with all the others, had a quality of human involvement and liveliness that later compartmentalisation of activities has lost. There would have been no 'new town blues' in such crowded places. Various elements are being taken apart to find the essence of good living. Is it the street, with all its qualities of coming-together — the reference point of the home at one end and the town at the other? Is it the garden wall — at once dividing line and talking point? Is it the existence of centres? We may find a way of rationalising mechanics and living-patterns together to replace architecture. Alternatively this may be just another of architecture's many definitions.

The real breakthrough of modern architecture was its manifest spirit of freedom. A two-way movement could now emerge with buildings no longer just putting a shell round life, but drawing from it the inspiration for a completely new range of environments. The term 'functionalism' meant more than ergonomics: it reflected this new spirit. Sometimes, when a sufficient number of new buildings could be assembled together such as in the Weissenhof exhibition or the Stockholm exhibition of 1930, this breath of fresh air blew strong. The addition of movement to brightness (we must remember that the white or bright coloured, smooth, flat walls of

Johannes Duiker: Cineac Cinema.

modern buildings contrasted sharply with the typical eclectic and encrusted ornament of the early 1900s — 'Edwardian' in England for example) had theatrical impact. Such a quality must not be sneered at, since it is in the theatre that we are more alert to atmosphere than usual, and atmosphere is a strong constituent of an environment — architectural or otherwise.

In its assertiveness, modern architecture has found devices that at once combine new materials and techniques and at the same time make a theatrical point. The glass-walled

above: Gunnar Asplund: Paradise Restaurant of the Stockholm exhibition, 1930.
below: Bernard Hermkes: Flower Conservatory, Hamburg, 1959.

staircase has become one of the most typical: it takes a key occurrence in a building, and one which demands a basic break with the rhythm of floors; it throws this occurrence open to the passer-by, and makes the most of the imagery of freedom, lightness, movement, identity of a key point, and probably exploits the clever piece of concrete work of the stair. The balcony is another: here, the symbolism of breaking out of the restriction of walls and extending inside to outside is often combined with an emphasised horizontality. These two ideas are interesting in that they could not have been attempted without the invention of reinforced concrete and the metal window. Philosophically important as the inside-outside thing is (and we have already found a hint of it much earlier when the invention of the column made the continuous wall no longer necessary), it has only really begun its development. The Victorians had their conservatories, and we shall see that they were marvellous things indeed, but they remained as set pieces in themselves.

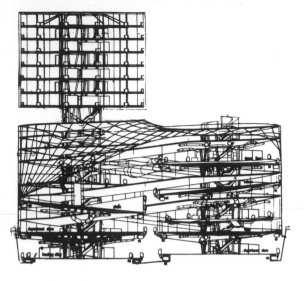

Erich Mendelsohn: business house, Breslau, c. 1922.

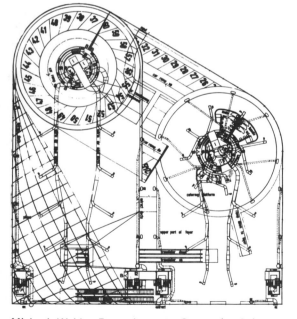

Michael Webb: Entertainments Centre for Leicester Square (project) showing coiled ramp and travellator system under draped glass skin, 1962.

The importance placed by the new architecture on the breakaway from the window as a set piece has close connections with the idea of the free plan; it takes the balcony condition as an opportunity to take this plan right outside the building and say 'here is our floor'. The long glass window, product of this same freedom, is sometimes regarded as no more than a rather tiresome incidental. In the Californian houses of Richard Neutra the climate does in fact allow the glass to remain folded away for most

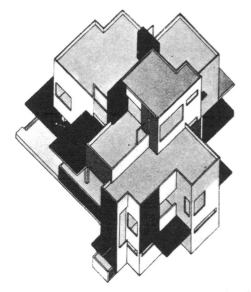

Theo van Doesburg and Cor van Esteren: project for a private house, 1920. An aesthetically conscious massing of planes and deliberately differentiated surfaces to form (almost as an aside) a usable building.

Russian constructivist sketch for an industrial building (from Tchernikov's *101 Fantasies*). Here again the direction and emphasised extrusion of the building and its structure are of greater concern than mere organization.

of the time and the inside-outside flow becomes a reality. Horizontality cannot be completely detached from the idea of speed and engineering assertion. The Russian Constructivists saw the drama of a new world not only in concrete but also in steel. Since their origins had also had much to do with the stripping of embellishment from the graphic arts (several of the Constructivist painters and architects were closely associated) the clear skeletal cages were ready to be remoulded. The spirit of 'Futurism', the name

given to a group of Italian architects and thinkers, notably Antonio Sant'elia, in the same period — about 1920 — was itself concerned with speed. 'Futuristic' became a popular label applied to horizontal windows in any context, to 'rising sun' decoration and to racing cars and, most of all, to streamlining. There is no doubt that the horizontality of modern architecture — developed from an art idea, and streamlining — developed from an engineering idea, hardened into a definite style.

Johannes Duiker: theatre and hotel, Gooiland. What at first appears to be a random juxtaposition of used parts does not fall into the trap of laissez-faire, since these parts are all sharing an original, but equally dynamic expression of the forces passing through them.

The history of the entrance hall or vestibule illustrates the way in which a traditional element, whose activity has not fundamentally changed for centuries, has absorbed different attitudes in architecture. It is by definition a key point in the building, and unique in the total organisation. It marks the transference from outside environment to the assertive part of the building. It may also be a reference point in the cage or network. In simple structures it may only be an elaborate porch; the effect of a symmetrical composition is to load it with an architectural punctuation which may be out of all proportion to its function. As the building becomes more sophisticated or simply bigger, the need for the cage organisation immediately gives the appropriate emphasis of function. Since it is now a unique space it can be given a unique feature. The vestibule becomes a domed chamber, with perhaps a staircase winding up within and helping to load its function. In Romantic buildings the control of light or outcrop into a tower might be attempted. In twentieth-century architecture this space has not been overthrown, it has been extended. The change-over from outside to inside becomes also the change from old to new. More activities are conjured up: it becomes exhibition space, waiting space and stylistically a dramatisation in which the character of the rest of the building is heightened. Only more recently has the concept of the city as a single building, or the large urban centre where one enormous structure acts as host to a number of independent 'buildings' within which much of the significance of 'entering' and the appropriate device will disappear. This is always likely to happen, and is both a part of the inevitability of change and an argument against the mere acceptance of historical *parti*. In these examples, the design of the building absorbs, controls, almost invents an occurrence. This facet of the total act of 'planning' has little to do with abstracts: it is highly conditioned by period, imagery and personality. The architecture of the past used a static language; the architecture of the immediate past has had to invent a language to absorb dynamic and change; it is reasonable to predict that the architecture of the future might actually embody this dynamic.

Much is spoken about 'scale'. Traditionally, it has been thought that there is an appropriate scale for functioning parts. From the most primitive level of the height of a man determining the height of a door, to the highly complex calculations for the intensity of light determining the depth of a room, the standard has been the human being, more or less as found. But the invention of the building itself creates a situation for man not quite as found. The invention of the lift, the double-glazed window, efficient heating and ventilating, hydraulics and the air curtain are such conditioners that the digital ideas of the past are no longer valid. But with this overthrow of understandable symbols there comes a justifiable unease in the onlooker. The most exciting buildings of the last half-century have most often been condemned as 'inhuman'. This inhumanity feeling is proof of the power of association in design.

The whole business of control of activity is something that can be 'tuned'. Space is not merely dimensional. The turning of a corner is a piece of architecture. To intensify the atmosphere of a room we lower the ceiling and permit more people to the square yard than usual. To impress, we raise the ceiling height and make the proportions of doors and windows suitably large. This is elasticising at the simplest level, but the complex conditions of cities make control of areas of movement, noise, quiet, an aspect of the general engineering. In the village each thing has its place: the church, the churchyard have a relationship easily related to the green, the high street, the pub on the corner. The number of variations of position don't seem to prevent us from understanding the significance. We are back to the structuring problem again. In a simpler organisation position is less important than symbolism of parts; the corollary is the complex location where there are probably too many elements for them to have any symbolism (they may all be new anyhow), so that the network cage becomes important perhaps as a symbol as well as a mechanism.

We can now begin to chart our experience of buildings and find that this is highly coloured by the conditions to which we are used. This may explain the preference for traditional appearance; in architecture familiarity breeds comfort. The speed of assimilation may have something to do with this.

Place	HOME
	WORKPLACE
	SITUATION
	OCCASIONAL POINT
	TRANSITORY POINT

Feeling	BELONG
	ASSOCIATE WITH
	USE
	RECOGNISE
	GLIMPSE

Quality	EXTENSION OF PERSON
	ENCLOSURE
	ATMOSPHERE
	IDENTITY
	VIEW

I. Zoltovskij : central power station, Moscow, 1927.

Of course this chart is a generalisation, but it does underline a similarity of degree between places as we experience them and the way we recognise them. Let us take a few examples. A restaurant which we use from time to time is a situation with an atmosphere which is peculiar to itself, though not personal. As it is relatively transitory, compared with the home, we can tolerate a heavier decoration, louder noise, more hybrid condition than we would like to live with. The other conditions can be more extreme. The transitory object may be a landmark or a place where people are enclosed but in transit. In either case it does not have to sustain itself for as long as even the restaurant, but in order to register in our consciousness at all it may have to be a stronger image. This is now being recognised in the design of airports and motorway furniture. The latter has completely exploded the idea of scale and registration of symbols relative to human scale. They are seen at such speed that they have had to achieve a new scale which relates their size to this speed. The landscape too has to be scaled up accordingly. Architecture now has to adopt this concept from the younger art of advertising design.

This idea does not apply only at the receiving end; we can turn the mechanism back on itself and determine the relevance of buildings in their ability to use place, feeling and quality. There is no formula; the brilliant building is probably the one that inverts the logical relationship, but knowingly and with artifice rather than with slovenliness of intention.

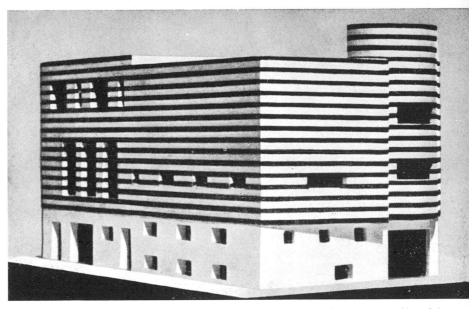

above: Adolf Loos: house for Josephine Baker, 1928. The effect of mere eccentric striping is to make this building many times more assertive than it would be in a more regular texturing.

below: David Chapman: shopping centre at Norwich (project) 1962. Cutaway perspective showing the integration between a repetitive prefabricated structure and a system of infilling storage racks.

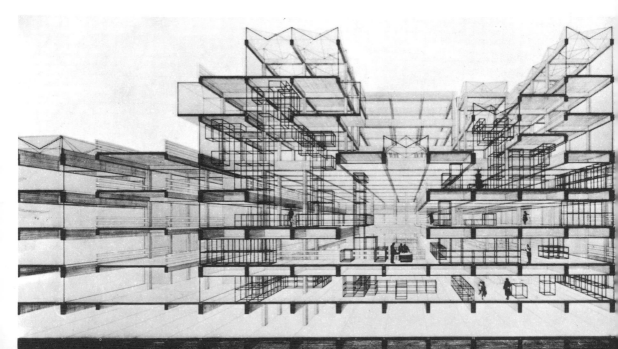

1

2

TOWERS.
left to right: 1 : oil refinery structures : exceptionally
dynamic in appearance and absolutely direct in function.
2 : Peter Cook : entertainments tower for Montreal, 1963.
A vertical city of three outcrops clustered around a major
spine with a systematized sub-structure of changeable-
use areas.

3   4   5

3: Nikolay Diulgheroff: tower dedicated to the victory
of the machine, 1930. A symbolic and highly formalized
neo-futurist structure.
4: Arthur Quarmby: tower of structural plastic units
free-form in plan.
5: Vo Toan: car-parking tower.

COUPE

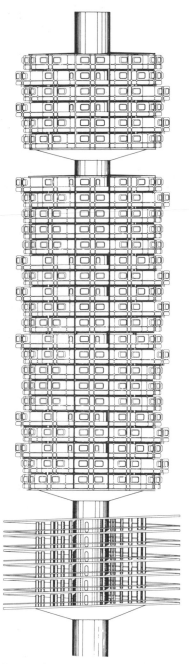

Warren Chalk: Capsule homes tower, 1964. A stack of changeable pre-formed living units around an access core.

Sam Rodilla: towers at Watts, California. A dream-structure realized by an inspired innocent.

The town originates at the bridging-point on the river while the castle is at the strategic point above and the inn abuts the highway. Inside the castle the keep is innermost and protected. The earth and timber castles are replaced by stone buildings which at first retain the basic organisation of one or more lines of obstruction and then the stronghold. The more sophisticated material permits refinements: bastioned corners, crenellation to permit the shooting of arrows, apertures to permit viewing and waste disposal. More subtle positioning of towers develops, one for each vulnerable angle. Gatehouses, buttresses, walls battered especially for various conditions

Deal Castle.

of surface, angle and defensive position — architecture has come out of the dark ages and is involved again in the art of planning parts based on technical know-how.

In churches of the same period, exact positioning is based on a liturgy with demands as exacting as the needs of defence. To trace the increasing complication of planning is to record increased subtlety based upon a multiplication of materials and techniques. Apart from the necessities of human size and social overtones the architect now has to manipulate the exact mixture and see where and when it occurs.

A fundamental device of abstract composition is to introduce into the regularly pulsating surface the one odd item, the red spot into the otherwise grey painting. Then comes a greater subtlety — the musical counterpoint of two melodic lines implying that both have perhaps equal weight or mass of notes. The art of pattern is one of the oldest recorded — it is the juxtaposition of two or more devices which may or may not be of equal weight. Renaissance architects were very keen on such things as rhythmic disciplines; allusions to music have been given to the Palladian A-B-A or more complex A-B-A-B-C-B-A-B-A. Apart from abstracts, the necessities of feeding-in the occasional item into the regular is to be weighed against the tradition of 'necessary' positioning such as in the castle. Rhythms are suggested by the mathematics of blocks of stone and size of things. Only at the time when the choice widens does there come a polemic between functional planning and aesthetic positioning.

Town planning in the seventeenth and eighteenth centuries was the art of positioning the odd occurrence against the repetition of terraces. The cage of streets could be mathematically regulated as in Georgian London, or art/

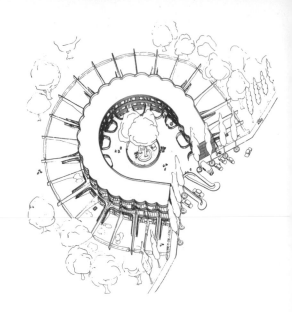

John Outram: motor-way housing settlement (project), 1961.

topographical as in Bath. In either case the architect's imagination was clearly captured by the placing of the square and the pedimented house at the centre of each terrace (as in London) or the bending of the standard terrace into an occurrence of its own (the Circus, Crescent at Bath). We must not be taken in, however, by the appearance of much apparently 'casual' planning. The formal quality of Georgian planning is clear: after all it springs from the formalism inherent in the rules for the parts themselves. Eventually, as a reaction to this compositional method, architects looked backwards to the genuinely random medieval town, or the building that had grown by the addition of bits and pieces over time. The Romantic revival in the nineteenth century emulated this casualness in single buildings. In the present century it can

W. M. Dudok: Lorentzweg school, 1930. An almost brutally simple and disarmingly direct planar building. Charming in its banality.

be seen more clearly in the ragged organisation of housing layouts and some otherwise highly organised buildings of the late 1950s. Controlled randomness is not necessarily the antithesis of a tidy mind. Many architects regard the ability to make a building of great sophistication and controlled intention, with the apparent quality of randomness, as a very advanced state indeed.

Against this is the continuance of the Formal tradition of the eighteenth century which also contributes strongly to the development of modern architecture. Such a building as Gropius's and Meyer's *Deutscher Werkbund* exhibition hall breaks into an entirely new-looking architecture with its now-famous corners and horizontality that must have been frighteningly different in 1914 although its plan is still axial and even monumental. This same is true of Wright's Mid-

way Gardens. Formal equation and balance remain today in the typical Skidmore, Owings and Merrill office block and the conceptual origins of such buildings can be seen in the Renaissance.

A very conscious attempt to break the formalism of symmetry came as a by-product of the breakaway in the 'twenties of this century. Asymmetrical balancing out was obtained by taking the major blocks of a building and disposing them about as one does with a piece of sculpture, and making sure that the 'composition' arrived at rose and fell. Dudok, at his peak in the 'thirties, was a master at this game (and really it is only an aesthetic game and as much contrivance as the symmetry which it was intended to bypass). The connection through the Dutch de Stijl movement to the formal experiment in painting and furniture is known to have been very close.

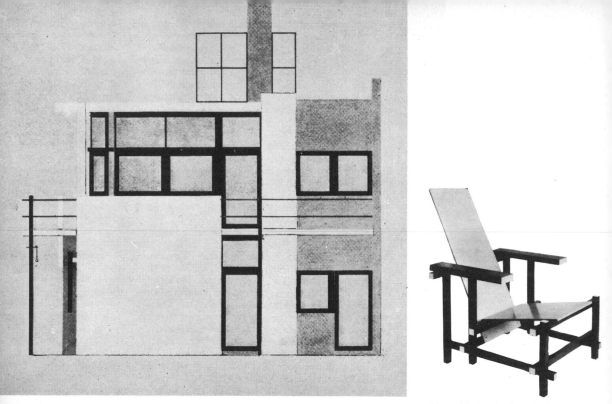

Rietveld : Red-blue chair.

The adroitness which many of the key modern architects have had in the resolution of whole buildings as compositional elements springs from the training that many of them had as designers of smaller objects; they had come to grips with the organisation of three-dimensional objects simply, and with an assurance that made them feel able to do away with the mechanical prop of the 'master plan', followed by a working down of scale in the traditional way. The contribution of the early period of modern architecture may well be seen in the future as its two-fold originality: the exploitation of free space (realising an ability that could have been achieved earlier, but was not) and an ability to plan in three dimensions.

As with the central irony of achieving consistency, the ideals of location do not always coincide with those of composition or structure recognition. Which is the better building : that which asseses the merits of appropriateness according to all qualities at every point and ends by being the most justifiably 'right' but is a mess ; or that which sets an ideal concept of order and consistency and bends the rest of the demands slightly as it comes to them? Such a battle goes on inside the architect's mind until the time that he has a fixed attitude, by which time he is probably no longer thinking very honestly.

The tests of position can be equally applied within the building itself. Rigidity of control is often seen to have broken down at some point

opposite left : Gerrit Rietveld : Schroeder House, Utrecht, 1924. Elevation drawing showing a very close analogy both in technique and formation with the painters of the de Stijl movement.

Hans Poelzig : Capitol theatre, Berlin, 1921. Typical of his expressionist phase in which a heavy (and highly contrived) mood hangs over the spaces.

in scale. The central idea of the duplex apartments that culminate in the Unités is freedom of organisation and positioning. The total cage of the building, on the other hand, is highly determinate. In this case it is at the front door to the dwelling that the discipline changes. In other places, the positioning of structure and access is very determined, but the location and size of rooms and the profile of the building is loose. The release of organisational control at a key point is a very sophisticated method of designing; it is rather like a puppet master who is holding all the marionettes but only jerking the arms: because the legs are not jerking we must not assume that they are out of control: they may be more effective if allowed to dangle with the strings still there. In this situation, it is difficult to test the building against one set of rules only, and any clues to points at which one set of values is relative and another stops need to be read.

The structure line, if there is one, is a useful point to start. Let us take the typical wall condition — is it attached? Slung between? Or does it sweep in or out? What is the typical relationship of rooms? Do they generally stop in one line? Are openings always in the same sort of place? What about ancillary rooms (a good give-away these) — are they always at the rear, in front, or between major rooms? Do similar rooms (in terms of size, or perhaps use) get put together in batches? Sooner or later, even in a Hans Scharoun building, one hits upon a situation which repeats itself. With two or more such lines of consistency located and a careful look at how functioning parts tie up with these, the way in which the designer saw the building can be plotted. Sooner or later we realise that many of the gambits he played originated in other buildings; they are 'type solutions', where the problem of function and consistency had been solved by someone else for that particular situation.

Objects which we can hold in the hand may look the way they do for a variety of reasons which have little to do with usefulness; as consumer products they are probably only sitting there in our hand because they have gone out of their way to make themselves attractive. These will be disposed of when we have tired of them. On arrival, they were probably in containers, neatly arranged for minimum packing space. We will disarrange them, randomly and according to some particular wish (think of a box of chocolates), until eventually the whole thing becomes waste matter, and is disposed of perhaps slightly less neatly than it came. While in use, the object has to do a little to make itself accommodated by the rest of the environment. Little benefit would be obtained by having a spherical container for most things: it would roll around, and therefore be uncontrollable. Most small objects are flat-bottomed, but equally, we have to provide some surface within the room which can accommodate this small flat object along with all the other small flat objects that we might like to have around. Furniture is the collective device for this — immediately we have a two-way interaction set up; the small item can have its own set of rules and requirements, and so too does the furniture. They have to interact; not all the furniture, but one has to bear in mind the ergonomic limits of the small object, and our ergonomic limits in relation to both. Most of us do not go as far as the painter Mondrian, who had such a perfectionist aesthetic sense that he would take an ashtray away from a guest and replace it in the exact spot which it occupied in the composition of the room, since all the furniture, objects and

Erich Mendelsohn: Kurfurstendamm Cinema, 1928: surely the prototype 'thirties cinema interior.

decorations had been neurotically and finitely postioned.

In general, the smaller objects need only to be controlled by our own day-to-day requirements, and the pattern of our life determines the general range within which that part of our environment exists. The effect upon a room when there has been a party and the normal environmental limit has been passed is well known — in fact the basic architecture has not changed; perhaps the items of furniture are the same, but their positioning is unusual; there is a higher level of litter: the schema has been changed. Buildings of the simplest form contain the room-type which has evolved from the primitive 'chamber'. Small, basic furniture is used in a fairly fixed relationship with the room. The recent spate of university building has been unable to take study-bedroom design far beyond the traditional monk's cell: sleeping function taking up one wall, the other functions distributed round the residual space. Even here, the treatment of the outer wall — its windows, the amount of opening-out, closing-in, adaptability, and the possible mobility of even as large an element as the bed — could break open this stranglehold. It is useful to take a look at the newer tradition of caravan planning. Confined dimensions offer no restrictions to change of environment from 'lounging', 'living', 'working', 'sleeping' with all the required connotations and equipment in the same space. The locational design of the last-named is ingenious of

above: Antonio Gaudi: Apartment interior, Casa Batillo, Barcelona, 1905.
below: Le Corbusier: sketch for an 'ideal apartment'.

necessity, but it is the concept as well that is worth noting: the greatest freedom within the smallest physical limits.

The way of dealing with the traditionally more important main room is to allow a hierarchy of positioning to enter into the placing of things, and the placing of oneself as well. This persists in the idea of the 'dining alcove', the fireplace or TV corner as focus, the most comfortable chair located in the most comfortable (best lit, least draughty etc) spot. The baronial hall, with its musician's gallery, high and low table and the rest, is simply a different interpretation. Modern architects have been faced with the interpretation of a seemingly free architectural space into a series of fixed areas that happen to be in one overall space. Architecture does not leave off with the walls, and ideally there should be some carry-through of ideas either from the building down to the design of the chair and carpet, or upwards from an idea of the range of living possible and the shell of the room made to obtain it.

The large space containing pools of activity is at best yet another method of internal environment-making. Frank Lloyd Wright experimented in the Larkin Building, where five storeys of office floor sit on either side of the nave-like central space. At once the 'local' area is part of the whole and yet defined, though not by the usual wall. Much later, in the Johnson Wax Company's offices, there is a large open office floor surrounded at a higher level by a single balcony of other office accommodation. The lower part is in fact a similar idea to the later *Büroland-schaft* principle of the creation of a large, flexible space into which the office departments are scattered with the minimum of walls. This development relies on the much more sophisticated control that is now possible over sound transmission and the ability to distribute electrical and other communication services over a large area. The *Bürolandschaft* implies a much higher degree of organisational freedom, and in this way is somewhat analogous to the cities of the future which will almost certainly be in the form of a single environmental enclosure that eliminates the problems of climate; the 'buildings' will then be free to organise themselves rather as the departments of an office or areas within a single building do now. The human sensation becomes complicated, however, since beyond a certain size of room agoraphobia sets in (at least such a lessening of association with the enclosing surface that one is instinctively unhappy). It is not purely post-

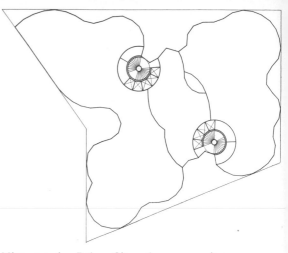

Mies van der Rohe: Glass skyscraper, plan.

Freudian thinking that lends support to the analogy made between the 'chamber' type of room — that which encloses one closely, is not exposed, and has plenty of solid wall around one — and the womb. Latterly, this thinking has led to the concept of actual womb-like shapes for rooms. If no more, there is safety implied in solidity and enclosure.

In this dimension, the nature of the wall itself is important: it has been found that the normal depth of a room from outside wall (arrived at by equating the height/depth ratio with the external light situation) must nowadays be exceeded in such buildings as department stores and office buildings. Artificial light can be sufficiently mixed (tungsten with fluorescent etc.) for such spaces to be tolerable. Eventually though, claustrophobia of a kind sets in if you

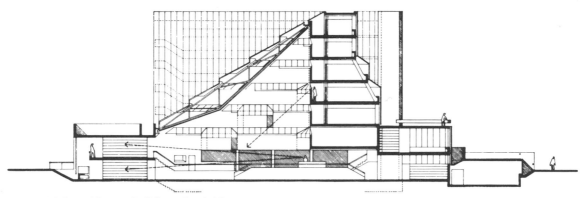

James Stirling: History Building, Cambridge.

eliminate all the windows. A 'viewing' window is introduced in factories, not as a light source, but purely to deal with this problem. In department stores the compensation of interest in the centre seems to make this device less necessary. We are now confronted with a complex set of situations: not only has physical organisation little to do with the problems of large spaces, but the type of design which allows for human weaknesses must be aware of several influences and counterinfluences. It cannot be assumed that the architecture of the building is so staggering that the inmates will be quite happy with this alone.

The technique of the lead-on is one that can be traced to Ancient Egyptian temples, where the chambers became smaller and more unique the further one progressed (or was allowed to progress) until the ultimate sanctuary was reached.

Two or more spaces can be linked, so that although we enter one, the next is always beckoning. Another variant is the grouping of several chambers (or even quite large halls) with one side of each opening up into the other. This again has the Larkin Building quality of all belonging, yet all being definitive. It is conceptually one of the most dramatic forms of interior — cathedrals use it.

How far is this from the fingering of a small object and the placing of it on a shelf? The architect runs through such an operation when considering the plan of a building, and the room is placed on a mental shelf ready for the next set of rooms to be brought along and computed, except that there are people inside; this interaction and humanity operates at every scale from the box of chocolates up to the design of the Regional Plan.

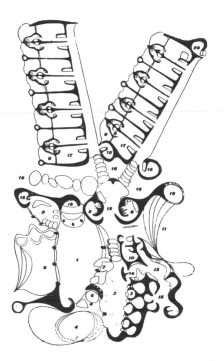

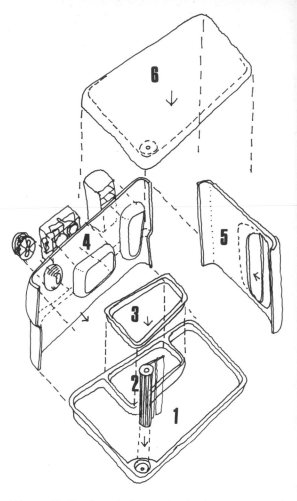

Pancho Guedes: Hotel (project), Laurenco Marques.
A highly expressionist and fluent series of volumes to be carried out in-situ, and therefore relevant in areas where labour is cheaper than any other part of the production.

Warren Chalk: Capsule homes (project), breakdown of prefabricated and interchangable elements:
1. Floor tray.
2. Roll-up wall.
3. Soft (bed) pad.
4. Appliance wall.
5. Internal wall.
6. Ceiling tray.

above: Victor Gruen: South-
dale, Minneapolis.
Typical of the developed shopping centre, an entirely conditioned and inward-looking environment.

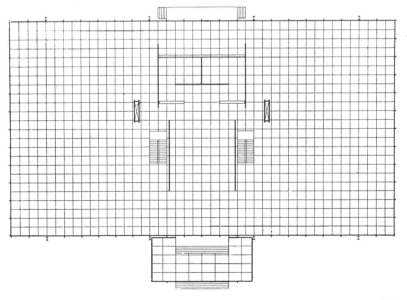

Mies van der Rohe: Crown
Hall, IIT, Chicago. Elevation and
plan; the most severe formal
rationalism.

Celtic monastry of Cashel and Clochan, Isles of Arran : the direct piling-up of stone. (Measured drawing by Andrew Anderson).

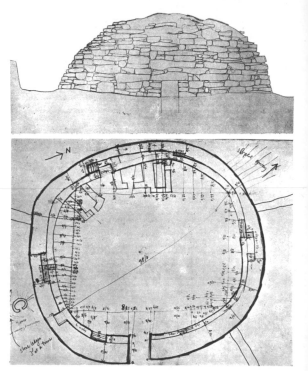

David Greene: Fully applianced house (project) 1966.

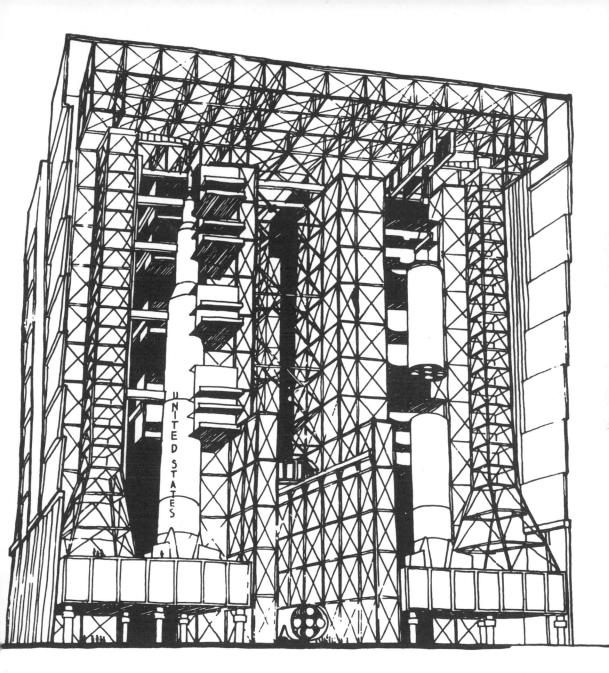

Rocket erection building at Cape Kennedy: architecture of the mightiest dimensions already beyond the brief of architects.

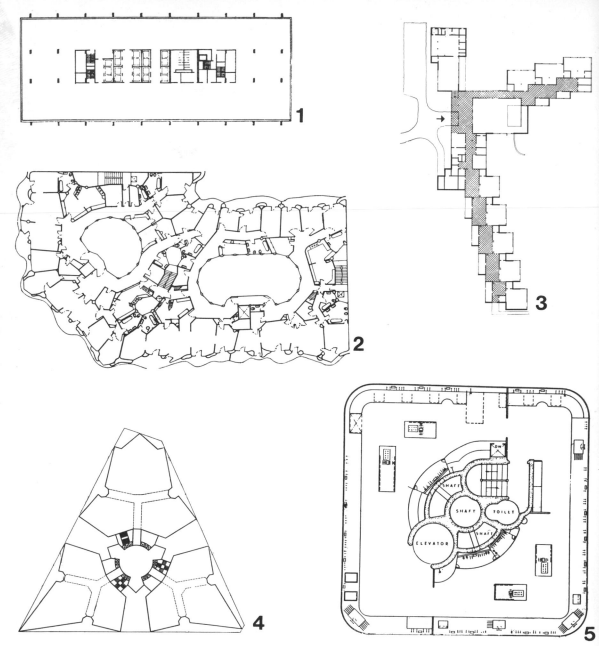

COMPARATIVE PLANS:
These drawings show very clearly the difference in organization and intention between widely differing buildings. Without the aesthetic discussion that surrounds the comparison of elevations, the nature of the architecture can be seen as more than skin deep.

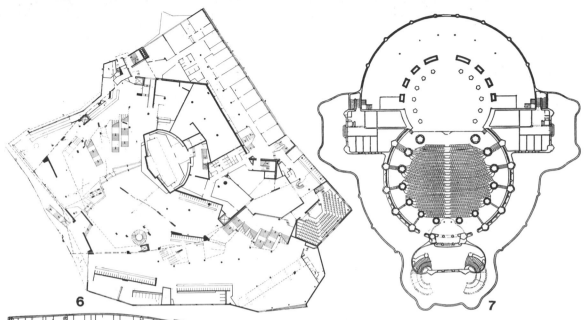

6

7

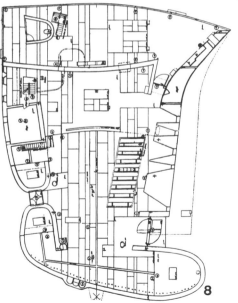

8

2. Antonio Gaudi: Casa Mila, 1905, typical floor. Very basically, the archetypical late 19th century mansion block organization, twisted and fashioned into a series of voluptuous surfaces.

3. Hertfordshire County Architects: Temple Wood School, Welwyn. A relatively scattered plan, designed to stretch the ability of the Hertfordshire architects' pre-fabrication system.

4. Mies van der Rohe: Project for an office building on the Friedrichstrasse, Berlin. Compare with the Chase Manhatten, above.

5. Frank Lloyd Wright: Tower block of the Johnson Wax building. The most advanced building of Wright, to that date (1936-39). The forms have a controlled voluptuousness, but the total organization is really quite controlled.

6. Hans Scharoun: Berlin Philharmonie, compare with the section drawing earlier (these plans are not to the same scale).

7. Rudolf Steiner: Goethenaeum (first building). The founder of the Theosophical movement was also a designer of considerable ability. This plan shows a very direct, big-scale handling of an assembly building.

8. Le Corbusier: Chapel of Notre Dame du Haut, Ron-champ. The familiar, but weird hilltop object is interesting in plan: since the geometry is clearly far more consequential than one might have guessed.

1. Skidmore, Owings and Merrill: Chase Manhattan Bank offices, New York. A clear and clinically rationalized ratio of useable space between central core and surrounding office area.

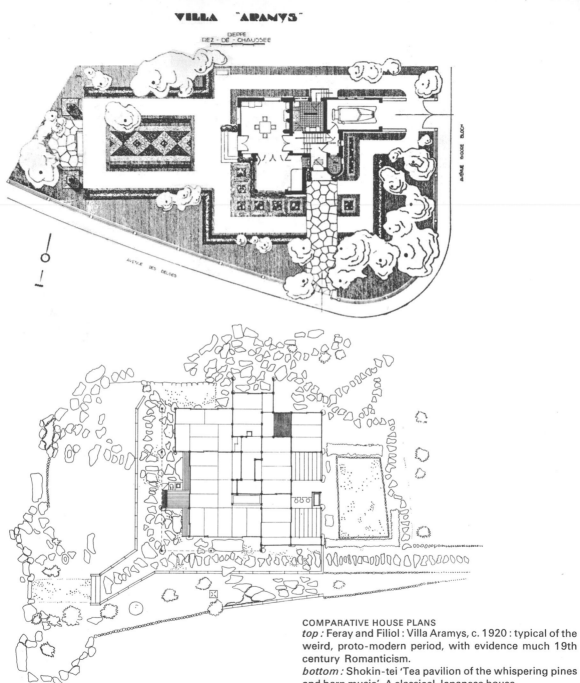

VILLA "ARAMYS"

DIEPPE
REZ - DE - CHAUSSÉE

AVENUE THEODORE BLOCH

AVENUE DES BELGES

COMPARATIVE HOUSE PLANS
top : Feray and Filiol : Villa Aramys, c. 1920 : typical of the weird, proto-modern period, with evidence much 19th century Romanticism.
bottom : Shokin-tei 'Tea pavilion of the whispering pines and harp music'. A classical Japanese house.

64

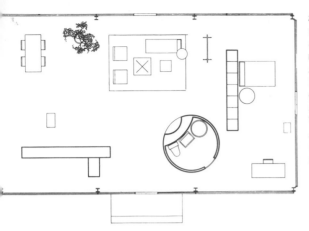

top left: Philip Johnson: House at New Canaan, Connecticut. A box of glass with only one small enclosure.
centre: Paul Bossard: House at Maisons-Laffite. A recent poly-wombic organization.
bottom left: Alison and Peter Smithson: 'House of the Future' 1956. Two units. Each organized around a patio garden. Built in plastic.
top right: Stirling and Gowan: House on the Isle of Wight, 1958.
bottom right: Marco Dezzi-Bardeschi: House at Florence (compare with the Bossard house: this is a much tighter use of curved areas).

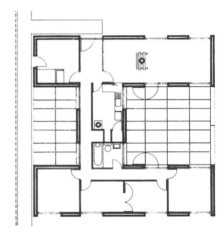

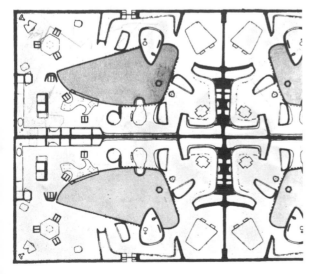

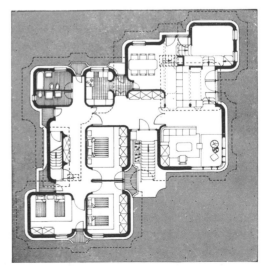

Big U.S. man-in-sea project

sea "house"—equipped with bunks, shower, phones, light and laboratory facilities.

above: Sea laboratory structure; another instance of the significant environmental experiments of today reaching far beyond the boundaries of architecture.

below: Peter Cook: 'Bat' plan house, first version. 1965. A free-form systematized house whereby a steel 'umbrella' frame carries the external skin and internal partitions. Central pylons disgorge the services.

below: Warren Chalk: Capsule home. (Plan drawing of the exploded kit of parts on page 58.)

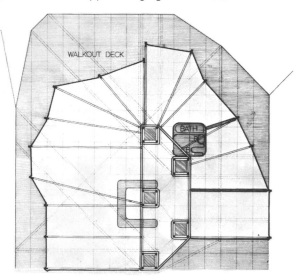

Gaudi's Sagrada Familia is formally aggressive enough for anybody; the activity built into its design is formal: it is part of an expressionistic desire to extract out of the placing of structure, weaving of space, symbolism and hardware — all at full pitch. The summoning of forces is Wagnerian in its might. In the Eiffel Tower there is tremendous power implicit in the scale of the forces involved; furthermore they are at work — and where there is no thrust or movement but just air. In the Kharkov factory there is as much activity, though it comes through a few masses with the tentacles only exposed on occasion: the rest of the tentacles are within. It is possible for as much dynamic to be contained in a seemingly 'passive' formalism. The debate about Expressionism will never be resolved. There has, at least since the late Renaissance, been a 'hot and cool' on either side of the architectural mainstream, one side holding that the parts of a building which are expressive of more than their mere existence should be demonstrated as working parts in some way. (At an extreme, even non-working parts). Every part if necessary should express its presence and its 'personality'. Against this is the argument that architecture is, all said and done, merely enclosure. This enclosure should be simple, obvious and efficient. The mainstream borrows bits of philosophy from each, expressing those elements which are potentially attractive, and

claiming 'simplicity' when it suppresses others that are less easily handled. Once again it can be seen that these arguments and counter-arguments can lead us into the dead end of 'style'.

Ultimately, the two ends are probably both nearer the truth than the middle. Architecture can never be the mere passive acceptance of bits and pieces of hardware, with the option merely of slinging them together and leaving it at that. There is a potential magic in the parts, and unless they are experimented with, their development is stunted. It can also be seen that architecture must at times express itself in 'doing' things: as pure communication; we need to know where we are in a building. Symbols, symbolic form and recognition are the means, and they need to evolve. Yet simplicity and efficiency are the basis of any sensible organisation and the whole consistency-appropriateness operation returns to them. There are, then, two kinds of active architecture: symbolic and functional. The corollary is that active and passive spaces can be created. In a building of any consistency, these become another stage in the interplay; we have already found this in as demonstrative a building type as a church. Elsewhere it comes close to the business of straight planning. In the chart of place/feeling/quality the degree of emotion and the time spent seemed to relate; we have seen that the size of the room has this emotional impact. Now there is the possibility of 'hot and cold' areas of the same building. This thinking is found on the city scale. The device of the square amongst regular (and for that time) high density building was not only a formal and philanthropic device: the outcrop of the square punctuates the tension built up by row upon row of building. The device of a narrow, quiet, cool lobby outside the large, light, active salon; the large, involved, dramatic active hall where business is transacted is surrounded and contrasted with small, quiet, introspective rooms where the real work goes on.

It is said that the world has entered a state of greater activity and movement than ever before. This can be seen in the proliferation of the obvious symbols: pylons, motorways, the aircraft, the factory, the sales lot. The advantages of present technology can be used in the other direction, though as it is possible to harness speed and energy for greater intensity, they can be used to develop spaces and devices of even greater tranquillity than the famous monastery garden. In the same building, within the same overall space, it is possible to simulate absolute quiet, enormous space, maximum enclosure. Activity may now be 'zoned' rather than caged within its own structure, and we shall have to discover the appropriate symbols. Perhaps these will be as dramatic and exciting as the fruitiest Baroque, and if they are there will be someone round the corner ready to 'rationalise' their newly-found symbolism into another discipline, which we shall have to learn to 'read' and recognise.

The instinctive or inductive processional through a building has long since been replaced by the necessities of industrial process, sequences that have to be followed for the building to exist at all. The production-line factory is the clearest example. Basically a linear organisation, all the building has to do is to place a shell round the places where an operation occurs. This is most often done by optimising rather than designing specific areas with a specific kind of shed. The need for an anonymous space is a current one when processes are changing, and it is very difficult to design around machinery which is only really understood by a few people and then, in bulk, is near enough the same as much other machinery. In times of material and economic shortage the idea gets around that it is wasteful to make a space bigger than strictly necessary; this is in a way a left-over from the traditional building system where another course of brickwork is clearly expensive since the system is paid for by volume of material used. Nowadays, system building has made the enclosure of large spaces by frame-and-sheet materials expensive only in relation to the number of parts used. The explosion of the 'exact-fit' space may really hit architecture when light weight structures such as the tensegrity domes of Buckminster Fuller, the air structures and the pressed paper skin sheds are around in sufficient quantities to be really trusted by everybody. Then, the anonymous shed will come into its own and, as we have hinted before, the 'building' problem will be that of subdivision.

The stringing-along of a predetermined process, such as that in factory or hospital or airport, leaves the architect's job as one of interpretation rather than inception. It may be that faced with a predetermined process his position as non-expert (as far as the process is concerned), but with a trained instinct for planning, may see past the accepted method. This is a new role, since until the nineteenth century virtually all architectural situations could be

Yona Friedman : Spatial City over Paris, 1963. One of the definitive megastructure-city projects.

interpreted right the way through, and the 'expert' was a rare bird. The enormous lengths of corridor between the kitchen and the dining hall in the great houses of the seventeenth and eighteenth centuries would completely negate the value of the plan in today's terms.

There does seem to be, from time to time, a shift from one way of stringing-together to another, and although excellent functional reasons are always evolved, they can be plotted over some years very much as a shift of fashion. The axiality and balance of the classical plan were followed by the 'elemental' system which was closely allied to asymmetry. This took the defined room-groups in a building as elements to be strung together, with overlaps in some cases, but always with the total box of the element being clearly articulated from without. A favourite device was to have a link between each element in the form of a smaller and visually weaker piece of structure. This is seen very often in the famous English post-war schools, where the stringing out of teaching units along a corridor of glass, the hall, the science block as an element and so on are not only appropriate divisions, but coincide with

the period in architecture that looked back to the Bauhaus and to the educational buildings of the 'thirties as models.

Recently, the fashion has moved towards linear organisation, not only where a linear process is involved, but for towns, villages, schools, hospitals, universities. In some cases there is a valid argument for this system, as opposed to radical, or close-grouped systems. Linear stringing is certainly appropriate where speed is involved, but is not necessarily appropriate to contained groups. The grid or mega-structure is another variant. Here, a series of lines of movement (usually two-directional) takes care of access, services, structure — all forms of movement. The rooms or (on the larger scale) 'buildings' are all infill, and require only to organise themselves within. The lines of the paths, corridors, streets, travelators, pipework and whatever may be organised on several levels; it is something like a three-dimensional tartan. In this way the running of a very complex urbanism can take account of change of use, expansion, of many different systems going on within, without the change or pulsation of one upsetting the progress of the others.

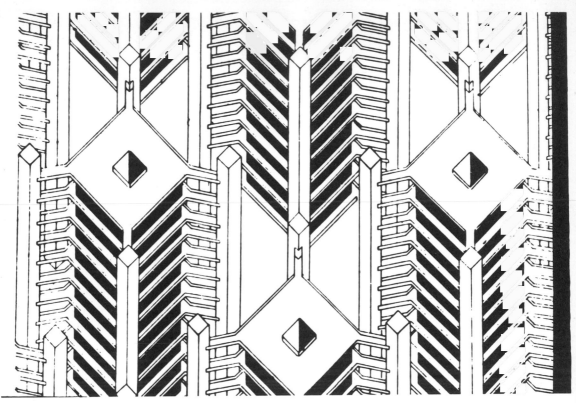

Theo van Doesburg: Circulation City (project), 1929.

This natural development of the 'cage' principle may well be the most appropriate for organising cities and large buildings now that so many overlaid patterns of movement and service occur — and occur quite differently with the development of the 'shed' in the ways that have now begun: new skin materials and system construction are the disciplines of the immediate future. Their abstractness in comparison with the disciplines of the past is probably their strength.

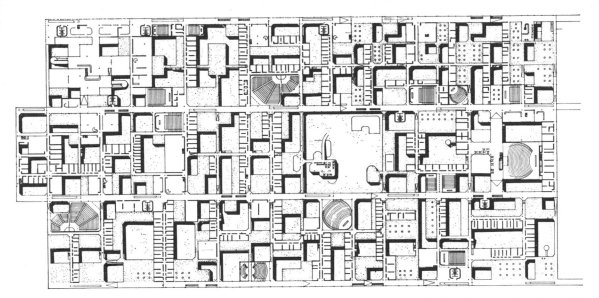

above : Candilis, Jossic and Woods : Berlin University, 1963. This multilayered system of a circulation tartan, infilled with a 'kit' of building types has had immense influence on the most recent generation of young architects. As with Friedman's project, it is a prototype of the most likely urban organization of the near future.

below : Hugh Wilson, Geoffrey Copcutt : Cumbernauld New Town, cross section and plan of town centre. The centre is a single building piled up over a roadway and lineally organised.

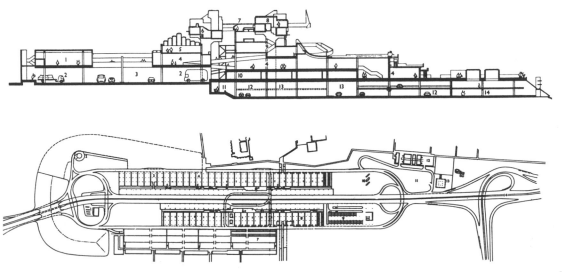

Guiseppi Terragni: Novocomum flats, Como, 1927.

opposite above: I. Golosov: Club building, Moscow, 1928.
below: Hans Hollein: city project 1963.

United Air Lines terminal, San Francisco. Moveable, telescopic corridors.

The psychology of movement has also to be harnessed. Railway stations and airports have the job of tapping a process line that needs to be fast, slow, active and non-active along its length, but always with the line of route to be taken made unquestionably clear. Signposts and waiting rooms are no longer enough. The development of the waiting-lounge bus instead of the long walk to the plane is simply a development of necessary architecture; the bus is now architecture. The word 'lounge' is just the nearest that comes to the function of sitting comfortably for a short period, but in effect the planned line is from terminal in the city to plane seat. Architecture is bursting its seams.

In shopping, the theory of the donkey and the carrot (and the essentialness of putting the

carrot right in front of the donkey's nose) is the basis of the organisation. The 'desired' goods are placed at the rear of the shop or upstairs, so that the customer has to pass as many 'impulse' lines as possible. The existence of a department store or a supermarket in the area acts as a scaled-up version of the same thing: if, in order to get to it, one has to pass many smaller shops, these will benefit from their 'impulse' interest. The shop hidden round a corner or made off-putting by being up some steps will do less trade. This area of planning is one of the most analysed and psychologically based of all, and can either be regarded as a prototype of 1984 or the first stage of really integrated design psychology.

Even in the home the housewife's eight miles a

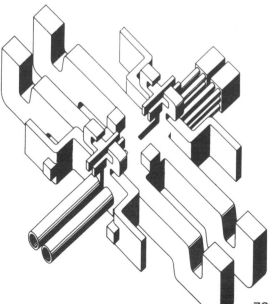

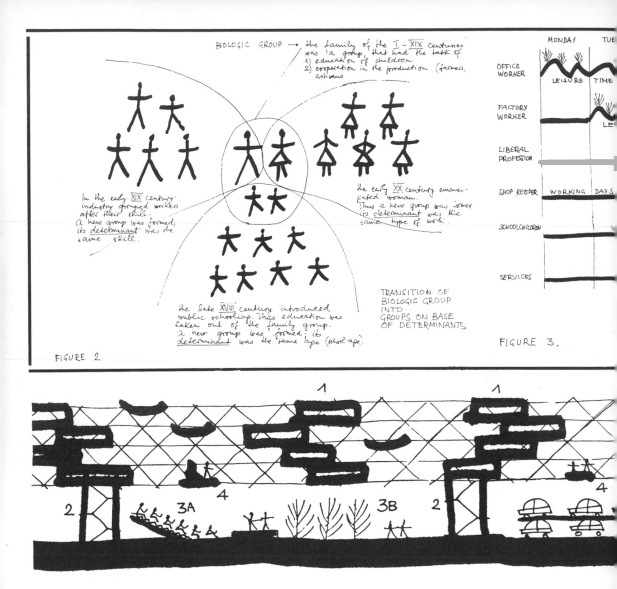

BIOLOGIC GROUP → the family of the I - XIX centuries was 'a group, that had the task of
1) education of children
2) cooperation in the production (farmers, artisans

In the early XIX century industry grouped workers after their skill. A new group was formed; its determinant was the same skill.

the early XX century emancipated woman. Thus a new group was formed; its determinant was the same type of work.

the late XVIII century introduced public schooling. This education was taken out of the family group. A new group was formed; its determinant was the same age (school-age).

TRANSITION OF BIOLOGIC GROUP INTO GROUPS ON BASE OF DETERMINANTS

FIGURE 2

FIGURE 3.

MONDAY   TUE

OFFICE WORKER   LEISURE TIME

FACTORY WORKER   LE

LIBERAL PROFESSION

SHOP KEEPER   WORKING DAYS

SCHOOLCHILDREN

SERVICES

day are a series of predictable process-lines. In kitchen planning these have been known and used for thirty years. The sequence of store-prepare-cook-serve- handle-eat-handle -stack-wash up-stack-store, and the many others involved in the kitchen, can be plotted first of all as abstract lines. The coincident points such as the sink or the working table are then related, and the circuit diagram so formed begins to look like a plan ; it does virtually become a plan when actual sizes of components are allowed to condition the diagram. This is a method of design which has become necessary now that so much of life is part of a process. It is also

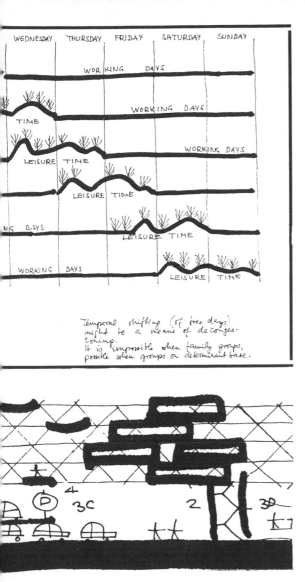

WEDNESDAY	THURSDAY	FRIDAY	SATURDAY	SUNDAY

WORKING DAYS

TIME

WORKING DAYS

LEISURE TIME

WORKING DAYS

LEISURE TIME

WORKING DAYS

LEISURE TIME

NG DAYS

LEISURE TIME

WORKING DAYS

LEISURE TIME

Temporal shifting (of free days)
might be a means of de conges-
tioning.
It is impossible when family groups,
possible when groups on determinant base.

Yona Friedman : Social balances behind the Spatial City (*see page* 69)

below opposite :

1. Individual utilization in the voids.
2. Piles containing vertical communication and supply mains.
3. a. Meeting places, theatre, etc.
   b. Gardens, parks.
   c. Department stores, etc.
4. Pedestrian walks, public and semi-public activities, bars, clubs, gossiping places.

below : Michael Webb : Furniture Manufacturers' Association (project) 1958. An example of 'bowellism' a student movement tracing its intentions back to some of the Romantic origins of the Modern movement.

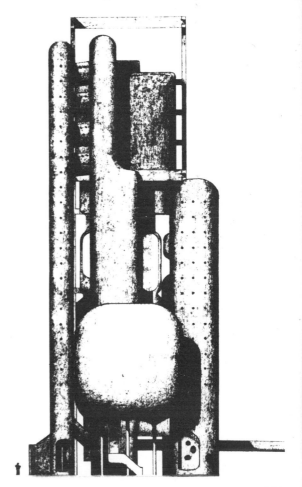

significant that it is close to the method of abstract analysis which the computer exists to serve. In this way the leap from instinctive design to some computerisation had been made — even before the computer was invented.

As with the house, the rationalisation of many (at the moment) subliminal operations is the

Paulo Soleri: 'Babel 2c' A 1700 metres circumfrance 'infrastructure for a city'.

City from an American 'Adventure-comix' strip.

largest step towards making architecture a science rather than an instinctive art.

As to the form produced by movement through a building, it is only recently that the idea of flow-and-form producing a continuous sculptural result has taken root. The unavoidable serrated outline of most buildings conceals the more river-like progression that a path of movement really takes. In complexes of buildings it is possible to relate them one to the other, so that the spaces between which are thoroughfares are 'tailored' to the intensity of flow or 'directioning'. The corner of a building can be eliminated (cut off or rounded) so that a path can run round the outside of it in something

Jiri Kroha: project for an office building, Prague, 1925. Early 'cool' functionalism.

more like its natural configuration — how many people turn a corner at a right angle? We all retain the instinct, even in urban areas, of taking short cuts.

It has become imperative for road patterns to be an exact reproduction of desire lines in fabric, and we see that certain buildings in which defined processes occur must have this quality built in. But where should a building stop? Before we know where we are we return to the old problem of expressionism. The deliberate throttling of flow is also a legitimate device of architecture: the picturesque tradition delights in the street that turns corners, the enormous flight of stairs. The Baroque delights in shuttered vistas, twisting routes. More simply, the device of turning a corridor about ninety degrees and perhaps turning it ninety degrees again back on course arrests the hurried flow — it makes an occasion. Running a corridor into a larger space (on the same path) is another form or linear occurrence. The sidelong view, the collection of several paths one above the other to be viewed from elsewhere, or to look out on an area: these are symbols and at the same time just happen to coincide with certain necessities — that of recognition again, and of mechanical simplicity.

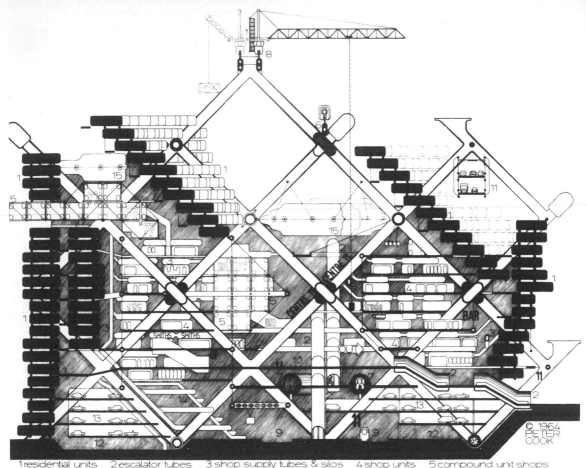

1 residential units 2 escalator tubes 3 shop supply tubes & silos 4 shop units 5 compound unit shops
6 fast monorail 7 local monorail 8 craneway 9 heavy duty railway 10 maximum circulation area
11 fast road 12 local feeder road 13 local parking 14 local goods sorting 15 environment seal balloon

above: Peter Cook: 'Plug-in City', 1964. Megastructure incorporating lifts and service tubes. Throw-away units.

opposite: Emilio Perez Pinero: Mobile Theatre project, 1961.

As with a natural organism, a building can be made to grow in the image of its smaller self. The advantage of a predetermined style was that any size of organism could be garnished with a recognisable set of objects; the actual size of these objects only became embarrassing when the human scale and these got out of control. A 'rusticated' base is appropriate three or five feet high, but when it reaches over the second storey of windows it looks ridiculous. Yet many

monuments have such anachronisms. If one can look at, say, St. Paul's Cathedral dispassionately, it would look just as right half its size, and would be possible twice its size. A need for subdivision arose with the growth in the size requirements of some buildings and the beginning of 'special purpose' buildings. The multiplication of gambits which still somewhere have a classical origin is the result. In the hands of a genius like Soane, this comes very close to a discovery of a modern architecture; elsewhere it leads to confusion.

The general method of addition was to build on more parts in the same style, but even if a more fashionable variant was chosen, the various string courses and entablatures had to carry through. Even in the twentieth century great store is set by the continuance of these 'lines' when adding to an old façade or a street terrace. Amusing attempts have been made in relating Corbusian concrete planes to pediments and string courses. The expense and difficulty of building in a stronger framework has limited the extension of buildings upwards, except in rare places.

All this has left architecture in a weak position historically for the absorption of the philosophy (and necessary practice) of growth and change. It has become accepted by planners, regarded without question by technologists, but has been a nasty pill for buildings. The technique used in cities of simply pulling down and building up again is too crude. A greater reliance on non-architectural elements of the urban crust may be the answer: roads and routes can define structural lines, even though the structure need not be fed in until required. The lightweight panel can allow the line of the external skin to be relatively unimportant in terms of weight, so that extension upwards ceases to be such a problem. The inflatable or disposable shed will mean that accommodation needed only in the summer, or for a limited period, need not take up any space at all: it is summoned up only as required. What is there to reassure people that all is well, what is home, what are the landmarks if growth and change affect cities as much as they might? Of course, there will always be landmarks; there are bound to be some monuments, and the whole urban structure and what

is going on within it will have to be much more clearly understood, so that the paths of change can be accurately plotted. There will have to be a hierarchy of change, some things having a long life-span, some a short. The prospect is exciting; architecture may return again to the position of really having something to give the rest of culture and daily life, instead of being an old left-over art that somehow has to be grafted on to the strange and rather insensitive world of technology.

If architecture remains by definition a static format, can it ever complement the mobility of life that is now lived? Cities made themselves able to embrace movement until the motor age, but so far neither single buildings nor the organisation of cities have really reached an organic method of formalising fast movement. Buildings which are involved in feeding or absorbing roads, airways, railways and the rest are generally adaptations of known static types with some 'flashgap' situation occurring between the (static) building and the (non-static) routeline. Even Victorian railway architecture, though it was quite successful when evolving a design order for such things as viaducts, engine sheds and awnings, was noticeably less sure of itself when it came to stations. The great termini which we admire so much, though they employ some of the best of the 'shed' concept for spaces in which multi-directional flow occurs, are nevertheless monuments. This can be seen if we analyse the difference of discipline in the organisation in the middle of the terminus, where factual matters, such as platforms, barriers and lines, are given priority and the edges (particularly the 'grand front') where pomp and style take over and the business of ticket buying, waiting, administration have a less functionally engineering over-tone — though they are just as much part of the sequence of operations. The result is high, draughty ticket halls, small cramped offices and meandering routes.

Of late, the need for mobility has been recognised; the speed and danger of vehicles has led to a popular town-planning device, the pedestrian deck. Buildings which are designed to fit against (or onto) such a deck refer their circulation lines to the first floor. It is in fact something like the *Piano Nobile* of the Italian *palazzi*. A second generation of decks is following; these will become linear and are really streets-in-the-air. The third generation will involve a two-layer deck, with perhaps two levels of transport below the pedestrian level, or an integrated system of services and transport. More and more layers can be expected as the idea of the city changes from that of ground with buildings on it, and the interactivity happening on this same ground, to that of a complex system of layers formed by the three-dimensional nature of buildings exploding outside. The buildings themselves, of course, will need to become more three-dimensionally organised. The services and the structure will no longer be a self-contained system. The city which is merely a single building may really be the outcome.

Points of transfer from one level to the next — stair, lift or escalator — have always been crucial. The first is simple, but becomes tiresome over two flights; the second led to the complete revolution of the city block — the limitations of simple layering. It may not be too much to draw an analogy between the future of architecture and the near future of automobiles — they will before long be indistinguishable anyhow — both prefabricated, both mobile? Both highly controlled in areas of high intensity, only less controlled in areas of low intensity? Both demand

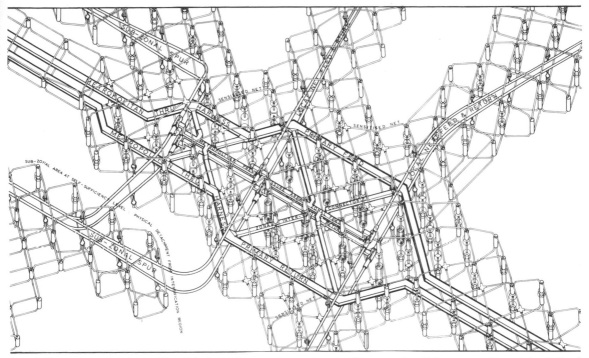

Dennis Crompton: Computer City. A balanced network of forces, interacting and changing. A sensitized net detects changes of activity, responds and feeds back information to programme the computer for reactions.

lightweight materials and interchangeable parts. Strangely enough, many of the lessons of the world of product design have only slowly come to be recognised as valid for buildings. It is certain that the future of architecture will be in system-building. It is in theory one of the bases of architecture anyway; the first wall in which stones of similar size were laid in a similar fashion was a 'system'. There was no industrialisation until the invention of the brick, where a material is deliberately processed to produce a standardised component. Once again it was the Modern Movement which found a strong analogy between industrialised and prefabricated methods and the symbolism of the new architecture as child of the machine. Gropius designs a body for the Alder Cabriolet car and is involved in the house system designed by Marcel Breuer at the Bauhaus. At this point organisational functionalism and organised production become fused as an ideal. Not all the functionalists subscribed to the prefabricated method; many preferred to see the image of the streamlined mechanistic object appear, and the grappling-point was left until the 1940s, when crash building programmes were committed to prefabrication. Somehow the aesthetics of the post-war prefab were psychologically tied to austerity and disappeared with it. The threads, now that they are being picked up, lack the determined quality which the prefabs had. The idea of system building has become confused with that of industrialised building, which was highly developed in the nineteenth century anyway.

Josef Hoffmann : Standard Steel house, Vienna, c. 1925.

In system building the design process extends beyond the normal range of assumption of methods before design and assumption of processes after design. Control *is* the design. The exact sequence of operations, the exact conditions, the elimination of chance form the first idea that there should be a system at all, the process of predetermining the number of operations involved in fixing a window pane : these are all as important as the strategy of the drawing board. The ultimate economy of means when the total process becomes the design factor

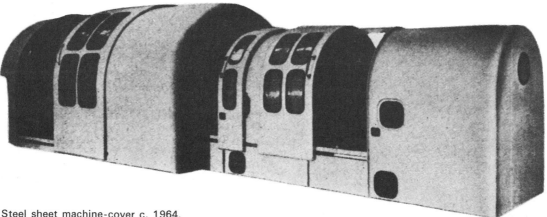

Steel sheet machine-cover c. 1964.

provides its appeal to thinking architects. The overtone of 'sameness' is merely the phase that we go through in any evolution in its early stages: the load-bearing boxes of the Mediterranean are as much the 'same' and for the same reasons: they follow a simple formula with few computes. It is the way in which this is then sited, extended, juxtaposed with the next box that appeals to many people's instincts for the picturesque. This is dangerous ground, but merely serves to show that we are perhaps being too pragmatic in our attitude towards system at this time.

The idea of buildings in this century being made from a million pieces, each stuck in place with glue, carried into place by hand, tapped and straightened with a hand-implement is too ridiculous.

One suspects that the architecture of the last twenty years has moved away from its earlier position as the reflection of public ideals and social symbols. Is this a lessening of affinity with the needs of the day or are we merely in a transitional phase between one set of associational values and the next? The 'locality', the 'home' and even the idea of 'place' almost certainly mean less than they did in the safe world of social division and narrow culture. The coincidence is not, of course, really coincidental. It would not only be false to rebuild artificially either the architecture or the society that held these safe, defined props; if our cultural explosion has resulted in an unheard-of standard of comfort and choice of experience for most people, this has so extended and scrambled the range of environments that such things as houses and cities have been left reeling. As we saw in the chart of experiences, time and conditions, transience works against assimilation and the environment which has meaning must go along with the relevant speed and fraction of life. Even the village now demands more than its pub, church and cricket pitch.

We may no longer be able to recognise at a glance the functional type of school from the block of flats; the style and the formation may be similar and still consistent with their needs. It would be too easy and quite wrong to attribute this to the economics or the technology of the parts. There has always been a current vocabulary which spans the range of building types. If architecture has become less definitive we must change our terms of reference, or lose track of it altogether.

We have accepted the fragmentation of methodical archetypes since the time when we became dependent on more than about half a dozen human stimuli. As a new artefact reaches the phase where it is generally understood, it is then referred to the nearest other artefact. The earliest carriage had somehow to miniaturise the salon. The railway had first to extend the carriage. Whether the artifice is simple or complex has progressively less to do with its extension into culture as it falls away from the creative into the interpretative stage of understanding. The early film recreates the melodrama; the later film seeks its own set of dimensions. The later film than this seeks to extend into mysticism, subliminal conditioning, education or whatever, and ceases to be primarily a film. The artifice becomes absorbed and its significance is turned inside-out.

Two propositions are now raised: did architecture reach this stage of re-assimilation in some past century (let us say at the point where the designer of a building fabric deliberately painted a mural on to the fabric rather than articulating the wall)? or is it only now reaching its true place amongst the rest as one method of creative

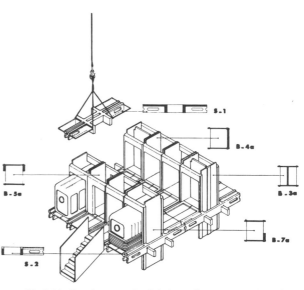

Noriaki Kurokawa: Prefabricated concrete housing, construction detail.

analysis? Is architecture self-contained by necessity or merely by tradition? We cannot avoid asking these questions when the intentions and the results of building ideas fail to communicate with the people who have to use them.

The ignorance of current design ideas is probably nearer to exposing the real situation. Architecture is no longer the mother of the arts, nor is it any longer the dominant method of organising cities. Zoning laws and highway engineering define the basic environment; architecture is its infill.

Yet the action and plan of buildings must retain their co-relevance. The wider context against which either actions or plans can be read is exploding. This is probably the most exciting stage that architecture has reached. The archi-

A heavy-weight Russian system using precast concrete.

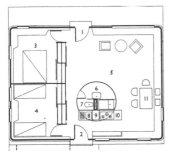

Jean Prouve : plan of experimental metal panelled house.

Le Corbusier, 1927 : Maisons Rurales, project for metal houses.

tect must now regard and create with an immeasurably wider set of values than hitherto. Likewise the observer of the architecture which is now happening must be ready for anything. The references are scattered, but the translation of values from action through circumstance to concept remains the basic process. Perhaps this is the process of organising or designing many other things which are not yet called architecture; if so it is the fault of our nomenclature. Once again, the method of the theatre, industry or education (a deliberately scrambled trio) is basically creative. The fascination of architecture is method and creation, not just the final objects. In this way it is the most explicit of artificial functions.

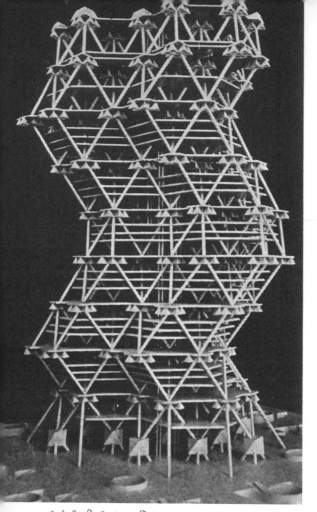

STRUCTURES ON PAGES 86 AND 87:

1. Russian constructivist project (from Tchernikov's *101 Fantasies*).
2. Konrad Wachsmann, 1950-53: steel aircraft hanger.
3. Russian constructivist sketch (from Tchernikov's *101 Fantasies*).
4. Konrad Wachsmann: perspective of a structural unit, 1953.
5. Gustave Eiffel: detail of the Eiffel Tower, Paris, 1887-89.
6. Charles Eames: IBM building, New York Fair, detail.
7. Constant Niewenhuys: New Babylon project, 1961, detail.

left: Louis Kahn: office building structure: project, 1954.
right: Noriaki Kurokawa: housing of prefabricated in-fillable room units, 1963.
below: plans and cross section of experimental steel panel housing project by Willi Ramstein, 1963.

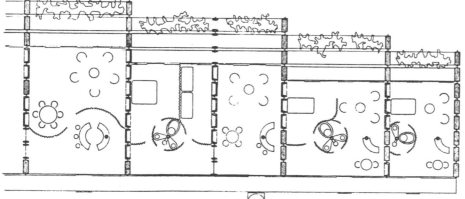

CHAPTER 5   THE BUILDING AS AN OPERATION

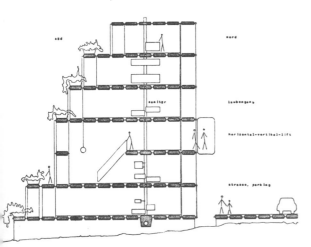

The process of forming the building comes from the abstractness of a series of ideas at one end, a series of constraints at the other, and any number of variable (and often incoherently devised) briefing points between. There is no ideal building situation, either geographically, politically or any other way. It is certainly true that the number of conditioners and restraints upon the straight line between requirement-concept-inception has multiplied with the sophistication of our society. The compensations for this outweigh its frustrations on the highest level, since it is now almost impossible to design a building that will fall down — and get away with it. Certainly it happens less and less often that the person who commissions a building is going to use it himself, less and less often that a single designer sees the whole process of the design through. With this dissemination of responsibility might come a time when architecture itself is the result of the optimisation of a series of equations, all based on formulae for the satisfaction of an optimised brief and for a group of persons unknown. Is this some kind of Hell or has it the logic of the inevitable? Fairly obviously the answer is both. The interpretation of these constraints, conditioners and abstracts is that they reduce the whole thing to the lowest common denominator. Another interpretation could be that the whole process must be taken to the technological limit, and the sociological knowledge which we now have must be fed back into architecture far more quickly.

In England, the typical building process still involves that traditional trio — client, architect and builder (or 'contractor', which is an elaboration of the same thing, allowing for the fact that he may well be an agent, hiring from other firms the necessary specialist tradesmen and craftsmen). The architect is in the ambiguous position of looking after his client's interests— and yet retaining the creative and professional isolation which can produce the best building possible. But we are culturally and technologically in a state of transition, and his role is becoming more and more ambiguous as the number of variables of control, technique and involvement of other specialists increases. The 'architect-cum-master-craftsman' could control the whole process, and therefore the quality of the building was entirely up to him. Now he must be much more the synthesiser, the interpreter. This might not ultimately negate his role — it just gives architects certain uncomfortable growing pains at the present.

Some of the most intelligent design is now being done by organisations who have architects, programmers, engineers, surveyors, technicians and the rest — all in one design organisation. Here the synthesis is possible while the concept is being evolved. It is likely that epoch-making buildings will continue to be evolved by very small groups — usually only one or two architects controlling the whole design. If we look outside architecture there are plenty of models for this; it is, in fact, the research laboratory situation as opposed to the production line. Its very hot-house atmosphere is probably necessary so that an intensity of ideal and ideas is not lost. These two situations are efficient, as is the likely extension of the 'off-the-peg' building, though at present the designers involved in developing such buildings have not reached a state of industrial professionalism, as have their brothers in the more traditionally industrialised areas of design.

At the other end of the world of architecture there is the continuance of far too many practices which were still possible when the need for sophisticated production-architecture was not so great: small outfits where the use of industrialisation is still a last resort when the 'handmade' is impossibly expensive, where people trained as 'all-round' architects grapple with amateur systems, amateur engineering and amateur sociology.

The typical building process starts with a briefing session at which the architect is given information about the use of the building and the financial limits by the client (or the agency, which may be a very complicated 'client' indeed — a committee of council, board, or a succession of heads of departments). In the case of the speculator, (especially with housing schemes and shop developments), it will often be part of the architect's brief to investigate the 'possibilities' of a site: in other words, to use the ingenuity of the architectural concept to exploit the maximum profit from a piece of land. In the past this would have been considered an immoral use of the talents of an 'artist'. It is now simply part of the sophistication of the whole environmental and building process in which finance can be made into a creative element of the design, rather than a restrictive element.

The next stage is traditionally the main interpretive and creative period in which all the abstracts are resolved into a balance — and a first-run design. This situation, the 'sketch-scheme', has always been popularly thought of as the time when the architect scribbles a building on the back of an envelope. This was not such a fallacy in the days when the first run could be thought of as a 'sketch'. The more sophisticated organisations will now use the early period of the design time for assembling and synthesising the brief: in other words, the balance of the abstracts is a scientific operation, and their choice cannot be left to the client, who is not a professional. This implies, of course, that the client has made as many sacrifices of his traditional 'pure' position as has the architect, in order to produce a better way of building. The brief will then be tested against various schematic models. If the firm has done similar work before, it will have arrived at a series of solutions for types of room, groupings and specialised details.

There is a danger here, of course, since if methods are merely repeated and not developed and extended we have perhaps a vernacular, but a dead and self-destroying one. For this reason, it is very necessary for the small 'experimental' architects to continue to exist, as they are always in a position to prove that the obvious, the usual and the traditional are no longer necessarily right. In the later stages of the design, the detailed work will follow upon the client's approval of the basic schema. The coming of 'off-the-peg' components has begun to reverse this order in some cases, and the job of computing and adapting standard parts evolved by some design team forms the main process. At some time, the design will be thrown out to tender, and a contractor chosen. Tradition has here reached full circle. Before the statutory constraints which we now have congealed, the architect and the builder might have been very much 'in league', but the emerging professionalism of the architect was designed to make him less corruptible (amongst other things) and definably the custodian of the client's interests. The increased industrialisation of the last few years has pointed towards greater involvement of all parties at all stages. Most architects who are involved in the technology of pre-fabrication and systems would prefer to have as close a contact with the industry as possible. This means giving up their professional isolation.

The actual emergence of a building out of the mud is almost an incidental point in the sequence of operations if the planning has been logical. The master-craftsman scribbling the detail of a moulding on the unfinished wall so that the carpenter could go on has disappeared. It is to be hoped that the constant amendment of details from day to day has also been eliminated by the synthesis of the design process. The building operation is a plan in itself. Exceptionally bad weather still plays havoc with wet materials, but this has become another argument for the pre-fabrication of parts, leaving the assembly as a 'dry' operation.

If the city develops into a changeable organisation of expendable building units, the old delight of the unexpected may return, but this itself will demand an extension rather than a diminution of pre-planning. Time and durability will enter the equation as well as all the rest. The architect will have to adapt even further. But the environment will gain; this is after all the ultimate purpose of architecture, rather than just methodology.

CHAPTER 6
FOUR REVOLUTIONS IN MODERN ARCHITECTURE

By this stage in the book, this should have emerged: one is basically confident that the explosion which happened to architecture in the heroic period (in the 1920s and 1930s) has led to an improvement in living standards. It has also led to a general levelling up of buildings of all kinds to a standard of utility and safety unknown before. Yet we have not realised the ideals of this century.

There have been three revolutions of ideas in modern architecture so far, and the fourth is upon us. These revolutions are necessary if we are to live not only better, but more dynamically. The first revolution had already begun at the beginning of the twentieth century. It was at first an instinctive feeling that beauty and the machine had somehow to recognise each other if the best was to be made of objects and buildings. When the white-walled 'high modern' emerged, this dialogue became interpreted as the symbolism of the machine as an abstraction of conscious design. Buildings were not necessarily to look like buildings: they had to symbolise the machine.

The second revolution involved freedom of the individual interpreted by freedom of space, freedom of the building itself, from the ground, or from conventional structure. Emancipation of people from formal conditions and emancipation of buildings from formal architectural conditions (as understood in the nineteenth century) went together.

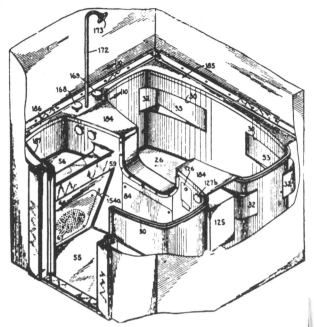

R. Buckminster Fuller: Dymaxion Bathroom unit, 1937.
(A steel prefabricated unit).

Teaching 'carrel' (individual, electronically-serviced unit), University of Southern Illinois, Carbondale.

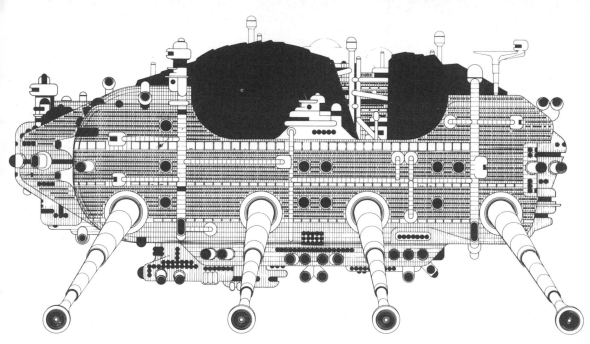

Ron Herron : Cities Moving, project, 1964. A concept of the furthest extension of grouped environment : a complete city that 'walks'.

The third was a revolution of context as much as of expression. Architecture was never again to be the same. It was to be as much determined by the state in which it had been forced to find itself. The demand was for housing for the people. The form, the Grand Design of streets, suburb, edifice, was from now on to be less the imposition of a total image than the amalgam of honest solutions to human conditions, added together and organised into a reasonable whole. The most definitive architects were as concerned with the exact condition of sleeping, eating, sunning oneself, as the play of shadow on walls. The revolution which will happen next involves the extension of all these, but more fundamentally the explosion of architecture itself into something much more equatable with the rest of our artefacts. Architecture will become infinite and transient. At last the dividing line between the things which carry around in the palm of the hand and the whole city will merge together as parts of the hierarchy of designed, phased, chosen objects ; to suit the condition and requirement of the time they will be able to be changed for something better. A total strategy has been seen to be more and more necessary as architecture and life become more sophisticated. The synthesis of operations in the correct sequence has more need to be accurate. The action becomes more part of the plan. Ultimately the user comes into his own. Does consumer choice of pre-fabricated living units and the like imply that every man might become his own architect?

A SHORT BIBLIOGRAPHY

The criterion used in this selection is the enthusiasm that is projected in these books. They all carry one beyond mere information into directions and speculations that cannot fail to be infectious.

FROM THE ARCHITECTURE OF THE PAST:

Georgian London: John Summerson. Pelican Book A574.

Summerson shows a developing architectural discipline and a developing urban environment meshed together and part of an enormous vitality. One can read well known places in London against their contemporary significance in economic, cultural and aspirational terms.

ON THE 'MODERN MOVEMENT':

Pioneers of Modern Design: Nikolaus Pevsner. Pelican Book A497

Theory and Design in the First Machine Age: Reyner Banham.

Architectural Press.

These two must be read in sequence. The first sets out the broad historical base of the struggle for modern design. The second is much more in the nature of in-group chat with strong loading that projects the struggle into the struggle of architecture with technology that is the love-hate situation in today's second machine age.

ON KEY FIGURES:

Le Corbusier 1910-60. Editions Girsberger.

A picture book, the bedside version of the more detailed 'Ouvres Complètes'. He was a genious of a kind, and the output should be seen as a whole. The progressions and regressions. The extremely wide range from paintings to cities. At several points during his lifetime, Le Corbusier could have developed into several kinds of architect.

The Dymaxion World of Buckminster Fuller: Robert W. Marks.

Reinhold Publishing Co.

The comprehensive review of Fuller's inventions and developments, which more than the work of any other designer, have pushed the frontiers of environment-making beyond architecture.

A CATALOGUE:

Encyclopaedia of Modern Architecture: Gerd Hatje (Editor)

Thames and Hudson.

A useful reference book with an enormous list of long and short essays, some are fascinating in their own right. An ideal refresher after a conversation with architects.

EXTENDING THE FRONTIERS FURTHER:

Fantastic Architecture: Ulrich Conrads and Hans G. Sperlich, Architectural Press.

The only book which so far collects together most of the experimental work in the first half of this century. Pictorially rather indiscriminate, its strength is in the letters and documents written by the early pioneers.

World Design Science Decade 1965-1975: R. Buckminster Fuller.

World Resources Inventory, Southern Illinois University. A strategy for survival by design and comprehension.

Inventing the Future: Dennis Gabor. Pelican Book A663. Basically about survival and the optimism of our continuing will to extend the range of our experience.

Profiles of the Future: Arthur C. Clarke. Pan Books XP54. Projections into the future by a famous space scientist.

REGULAR READING:

In England the two established monthlies *Architectural Review* and *Architectural Design* cover most architectural ground. The former is the less adventurous.

Edilizia Moderna published in Italy is probably the most exciting large-format architectural magazine.

Architecture d'aujourd'hui published in France is indiscriminating, but has a coverage of some of the most dramatic 'architects' architecture.

Archigram is a once-yearly effort, edited by the author, containing experimental work.

Most designers involved in the last third of the twentieth century keep abreast of the following: *Scientific American, New Scientist* (UK), *New Society* (UK), *Analog, Time* and *Paris Match.*

ACKNOWLEDGEMENTS

Special thanks are due to Dennis Crompton for his help with a large body of the illustration material. To Robert Vickery for his photographs of various buildings by Johannes Duiker. To Royston Landau for his photographs of the Rodillo Tower at Watts. To Tony Gwilliam for his photographs of various buildings by Antonio Gaudi. To the following architects who have helped with the selection of work for inclusion: David Chapman, Arthur Quarmby, John Outram, Yona Freidman, Konrad Wachsmann, Noriaki Kurokawa, Andrew Anderson, Warren Chalk, Ron Herron, David Greene, Michael Webb. The Friday Mosque photograph is by Michael Wilford. The photograph of Kidwelly Castle is reproduced by permission of the Ministry of Public Building and Works. Much material has previously appeared in *Archigram.* Other material has previously appeared in *Architectural Design* to whom thanks are due. All attempts to trace copyright have been made, but much material is from publications with originals of obscure origin.